Mediterranean Diet Coc

Simple Italian Recipes for Lose Weight and Live Healthy

Stephanie Flores

TABLE OF CONTENTS

INTRODUCTION

BREAKFAST RECIPES

LUNCH RECIPES

DESSERT RECIPES

CONCLUSION

INTRODUCTION

The Mediterranean diet is full of never-ending varieties of healthy, fresh, and delicious foods. However, there is more of an emphasis on certain types of foods, nothing is excluded. People who try a Mediterranean diet can relish the dishes they love while also indulging how good the tastiest, freshest foods can be.

The Mediterranean diet pattern, you will come closer to nature as the entire food concept depends on fresh produce. Mealtime, in these lands, is nothing short of a celebration. People, living in these parts have a tradition of eating together. It is time to nurture interpersonal relations as well.

It is the right time to get into the stride and do something that will not only improve your current state but will also gift you a healthy future. After all, there is no more significant wealth than the health of an individual.

Remember, it is safe to presume that the Mediterranean diet will help enhance a person's immune system. A person with a robust immune system will be capable to fight diseases easily. Therefore, your desire of leading a fulfilling, healthy and constructive life will be attained successfully.

The goal was to provide a thorough look at this diet and all the advantages and disadvantages it can bring to your life. As always, when making dietary changes you should consult your physician first to ensure this is a healthy change for you to achieve your goals in regard to your individual health. With the Mediterranean diet, much research has proven it is the most efficient method to lose weight and improve your overall health.

With this book, wanted to provide a detailed look at the Mediterranean lifestyle and exactly what it entails. The more informed you are about this diet and exactly what you should and should not be eating, the greater your chances of success will be!

People love incorporating a Mediterranean diet lifestyle because of how user-friendly it is! There are no counting calories, decreasing your portion sizes, or counting your intake of macronutrients diligently all day. It's about learning what the diet entails and making those choices to fill your pantry and fridge with fresh, healthy ingredients that will promote better health. You will be cutting out the unhealthy things like processed foods, artificial sugars, refined grains, and soda from your diet which is known to cause blood sugar spikes and excess weight gains. Instead, you'll be shopping for ingredients rich in vitamins, minerals, good fats, and antioxidants that will improve your health! With a menu allowing whole grains, fish, seafood, fruit, vegetables, and even a glass of wine a day, the Mediterranean diet allows for such variety that you can't get sick of it!

As long as you do this and stick to the simple rules of a Mediterranean diet, you can attain all the benefits it offers. One of the major benefits of this diet is that it is perfectly sustainable in the long run, not to mention, it is mouth-watering and delicious.

Once you start implementing the various protocols of this diet, you will see a positive change in your overall health. Ensure that you are being patient with yourself and stick to your diet without making any excuses.

Transitioning into the Mediterranean diet is mainly about bracing yourself for a new way of eating, adapting your attitude toward food into one of joyful expectation and appreciation of good meals and good company. It's like a mindset as anything else, so you'll want to make your environment unite so you can quickly adapt to the lifestyle in the Mediterranean way.

BREAKFAST RECIPES

1. Heart-Healthful Trail Mix

Preparation Time: 8 minutes
Cooking Time: 32 minutes
Serving: 12
Ingredients:

- 1 cup raw almonds
- 1 cup walnut halves
- 1 cup pumpkin seeds
- 1 cup dried apricots, cut into thin strips
- 1 cup dried cherries, roughly chopped
- 1 cup golden raisins
- 2 tablespoons extra-virgin olive oil
- 1 teaspoon salt

Direction

1. Preheat the oven to 300°F. Line a baking sheet with aluminum foil.
2. In a large bowl, mix almonds, walnuts, pumpkin seeds, apricots, cherries, and raisins. Pour the olive oil over all and toss well with clean hands. Add salt and toss again to distribute.
3. Fill in the nut mixture onto the baking sheet in a single layer and bake until the fruits begin to brown, about 30 minutes. Chill on the baking sheet to room temperature.
4. Store in a large airtight container or zipper-top plastic bag.

Nutrition: 109 calories 7g fats 1g protein

2. Citrus-Kissed Melon

Preparation Time: 11 minutes
Cooking Time: 0 minute
Serving: 4
Ingredients:

- 2 cups cubed melon
- 2 cups cubed cantaloupe
- 1/2 cup freshly squeezed orange juice
- 1/4 cup freshly squeezed lime juice
- 1 tablespoon orange zest

Direction

1. In a large bowl, incorporate melon cubes. In a bowl, blend the orange juice, lime juice, and orange zest and pour over the fruit.
2. Cover and cool for 4 hours, stirring occasionally. Serve chilled.

Nutrition: 101 calories 11g fats 2g protein

3. Café Cooler

Preparation Time: 16 minutes
Cooking time: 0 minute
Serving: 4
Ingredients:

- Ice cubes
- 2 cups low-fat milk
- 1/2 teaspoon ground cinnamon
- 1/2 teaspoon pure vanilla extract
- 1 cup espresso, cooled to room temperature
- 4 teaspoons sugar (optional)

Direction

1. Fill four tall glasses with ice cubes.
2. In a blender, combine the milk, cinnamon, and vanilla and blend until frothy.
3. Pour the milk over the ice cubes and top each drink with one-quarter of the espresso. If using sugar, stir it into the espresso until it has dissolved. Serve immediately, with chilled teaspoons for stirring.

Nutrition: 93 calories 7g fats 1g protein

4. Spring Caponata with Olives and Pomegranate

Preparation Time: 7 minutes
Cooking Time: 21 minutes
Serving: 4

Ingredients

- 3 ½ oz almonds
- 10 ½ oz olives
- 2oz celery stalk
- 100 ml olive oil
- 2 oz capers
- 1 ½ oz sugar
- 5oz raisins
- 50ml white wine vinegar
- Grenades 1 piece

Directions

1. Boil 1 liter of water with salt in a saucepan and stir in celery chopped into small pieces in it for two minutes. Drain the water, cool the celery so that it does not lose its green color.
2. Pour almonds into a frying pan and put in the oven for five minutes, preheated to 180 degrees.
3. Take out seeds from the olives and chop the flesh roughly.
4. Rinse the salted capers and chop them roughly. Roasted nuts in the oven are also roughly chopped.
5. Heat olive oil in a large saucepan, add sugar, capers, raisins, vinegar, a pinch of black pepper, olives, and simmer over medium heat for five minutes. Then pour celery into a stewpan and simmer for another two to three minutes. When serving, mix with pomegranate seeds and almonds.

Nutrition: 650 Calories 45.8g Fat 8g Protein

5. Smoked Salmon Appetizer with Fresh Cucumber

Preparation Time: 1 0minutes
Cooking Time: 0 minute

Serving: 4
Ingredients

- 2 ½ tbsp sour cream 10%
- 16 slices rye bread
- 3 tbsp Greek yogurt
- Dill to taste
- 16 pieces smoked salmon
- 16 pieces cucumbers

Directions

1. Blend sour cream and yogurt.
2. Put slices of rye bread on the dish (you can cut circles or squares out of them).
3. On each put a mug of cucumber, a little sauce, and a slice of fish. Garnish with dill branches on top.

Nutrition: 225 Calories 9g Fat 24g Protein

6. Cypriot Tomato Salad

Preparation Time: 13 minutes
Cooking Time: 0 minute
Serving: 4
Ingredients

- 4 pieces tomatoes
- 50 ml sesame oil
- 1 tbsp red wine vinegar
- 2 tbsp - dried oregano
- coarse sea salt to taste
- 9 oz feta cheese

Directions

1. Chop the tomatoes into slices and put on a plate.
2. Sprinkle with sesame oil and vinegar, sprinkle with salt and oregano.

3. Cut the cheese and put it on the tomatoes.
4. Allow the dish to stand for 30 minutes so that the tomatoes absorb spices and aromas.

Nutrition: 80 Calories 7g Fat 3g Protein

7.   Tangerine and Olive Salad

Preparation Time: 16 minutes
Cooking Time: 0 minute
Serving: 4
Ingredients

- ½ lb. tangerines
- 50 ml extra virgin olive oil
- 3 ½ oz Kalamata olives
- ½ tsp Ground cumin
- 1 tbsp White wine vinegar
- ¼ tsp paprika
- 1/8 tsp Cayenne pepper
- 1-piece Lettuce
- 2 oz Parsley
- Salt to taste
- Ground black pepper to taste

Directions

1. Remove the peel from the tangerines and remove the membranes between the slices (this can be done with a sharp knife, trying to touch the pulp as little as possible, or by hand, if the fruit is easy to peel). Put the naked slices in a wide bowl.
2. Olives (first, they will need to be removed from the seeds) cut in half and add to the tangerines.
3. Beat vinegar, oil, cumin, and paprika with a whisk in a separate bowl until smooth. Add the resulting dressing to a bowl.
4. Wash and dry lettuce with your hands to tear into small flakes and arrange on four plates, put tangerines with olives on top, and sprinkle salad with chopped parsley.

Nutrition: 173 Calories 15.4g Fat 1.4g Protein

8. Farfalle with Avocado

Preparation Time: 6 minutes
Cooking Time: 13 minutes
Serving: 4
Ingredients

- 10 ½ oz Farfalle pasta
- 5 oz Champignons
- 1 bunch Radish
- 1-piece Avocado
- 1 oz Parsley
- 6 oz Canned Tuna
- 6 tbsp vegetable broth
- 1 tbsp mustard
- Salt to taste

Directions

1. Cook the pasta.
2. Slice the champignons into thin plates and fry. Cut the radish into 6-8 slices. Cut avocado into slices. Finely chop the parsley.
3. Mix the broth with mustard, salt, and pepper, pour pasta on it.
4. Add tuna (previously draining the liquid), champignons, radishes, avocados, parsley. Mix everything and let it brew for half an hour in a cool place.

Nutrition: 125 Calories 3.2g Fat 7g Protein

9. Salad of Squid, Apples, and Green Peas

Preparation Time: 13 minutes
Cooking Time: 4 minutes
Serving: 2
Ingredients

- 7 oz squids
- 2 chicken egg

- ½ apple
- 8 ½ oz canned Green Peas
- Mayonnaise to taste
- Ground black pepper to taste
- Salt to taste
- Lemon juice to taste

Directions

1. Squids boiled in salted water (cook 3 minutes after boiling) cut into strips.
2. Finely chopped boiled eggs and apples.
3. Stir everything. Add peas and pepper. Season to taste with mayonnaise (can be sour cream); add lemon juice if desired.

Nutrition: 303 Calories 7.4g Fat 45g Protein

10. Three Bean Salad with French Sauce

Preparation Time: 4 minutes
Cooking Time: 11 minutes
Serving: 4
Ingredients

- 3 ½ oz Green beans
- 7 oz Beans fava
- 11 oz Lima Beans
- 11oz Kidney Beans
- 1 Red onion
- 1 tsp Italian parsley
- 2 tbsp French sauce

Directions

1. Boil slightly salted water in a saucepan. Put in it chopped green beans and fava beans (after defrosting them).
2. Cook for 1 minute, then drain the water. Fill with cold water, cool, and drain again.
3. Finely chop the small onion and parsley. Remove the beans from

cans and drain the water.
4. Stir all the ingredients in a bowl, fill with sauce.

Nutrition: 81 Calories 5.5 Fat 0.8g Protein

11. Sandwich with Tongue, Arugula and Champignons

Preparation Time: 16 minutes
Cooking Time: 0 minute
Serving: 2
Ingredients

- 1-piece pitta bread
- 1-piece Tomatoes flame
- 1 bunch Arugula
- 5oz Fresh champignons
- 1 tsp Truffle oil
- 2 tbsp Olive Oil
- Dried thyme to taste
- Ground black pepper to taste
- Salt to taste
- 3 ½ oz veal tongue

Direction

1. Chop the tongue into long thin slices and fry in olive oil, salt, pepper, and add thyme to taste.
2. Lightly fry the champignons in olive oil, put in a clean bowl, trying to leave excess oil in a pan. Drizzle with truffle oil to give mushrooms a flavor.
3. Put the arugula, thin slices of tomato, mushrooms, and tongue evenly on the unfolded pita bread.
4. Wrap tightly, if necessary, cut off excess pita bread along the edges. Cut into two and serve.

Nutrition: 200 Calories 13.6g Fat 7.5g Protein

12. Pineapple Raspberry Smoothie

Preparation Time: 20 minutes

Cooking Time: 0 minute
Serving: 4
Ingredients

- 1 ½ lb. pineapple
- 10 ½ oz frozen raspberries
- 300 ml vanilla rice milk
- 3 tbsp buckwheat flakes
- Mint to taste

Direction

1. Chop the piece of pineapple peel and remove the core. Cut into medium pieces.
2. Thaw raspberries overnight on the top shelf of the refrigerator.
3. Take 200 ml of rice milk (in the absence of it, of course, you can replace it with non-fat milk), buckwheat flakes, slices of mandarin and pineapple, and beat at high speed in a blender.
4. Let stand for about 10-15 minutes. During this time, buckwheat flakes will swell.
5. Add another 100 ml of rice drink and punch in the blender again. If the smoothie is still thick, bring the water or rice drink to the desired concentration.
6. Garnish with fresh mint leaves.

Nutrition: 45 Calories 0.3g Fat 8g Protein

13. Morning Cake with Oatmeal, Bananas, and Blueberries

Preparation Time: 18 minutes
Cooking Time: 33 minutes
Serving: 4
Ingredients

- 2 pieces Bananas
- 1 cup Blueberries
- 3 tbsp Honey
- 1oz walnuts
- 1 cup oatmeal

- 200 ml milk
- 1/3 tsp cinnamon
- 1 chicken egg
- 1 tsp vanilla
- 1 tsp powdered sugar

Direction

1. Prep the oven to 375 F. Wrap the bottom dish and sides of the foil
2. Cut the bananas into rings and put them in the prepared dishes. There we add half the blueberries, 1/4 tsp of cinnamon, 1 tbsp of honey, and cover with foil. Bake for 15 minutes
3. Then, in a bowl, mix the oatmeal, half the walnuts, the baking powder for the dough, and the remaining cinnamon; mix everything. In a separate bowl, beat the remaining honey, milk, eggs, and vanilla.
4. Get bananas with blueberries from the oven, sprinkle with an oatmeal mixture. Then evenly pour the mixture from milk. Sprinkle with the remaining blueberries and walnuts.
5. Bake the cake for about 30 minutes. For decoration, sprinkle with powdered sugar. Serve warm.

Nutrition: 83 Calories 2.2g Fat 2.5g Protein

14. Pita Chicken Salad

Preparation Time: 18 minutes
Cooking Time: 4 minutes
Serving: 4
Ingredients

- Olive oil 1 tablespoon
- 1-piece chicken breast
- 2 pieces pita
- Dried basil to taste
- 3 tbsp natural yogurt
- 1 tbsp lemon juice
- 1 clove garlic
- 1 bunch (7 oz) green salad

- 1 tomato
- 2 chives
- 1 cucumber
- Salt to taste
- Ground black pepper to taste

Directions

1. Rub the chicken slices with salt, pepper, and dried basil, fry in a pan until cooked.
2. Put chicken, salad, slices of tomato, cucumber, and onion in half the pits.
3. Mix yogurt with lemon juice and garlic, add to the salad in Pita.

Nutrition 94 Calories 1.8g Fat 6g Protein

LUNCH RECIPES

15. Red Pepper Hummus

Preparation Time: 7 minutes
Cooking Time: 34 minutes
Serving: 4
Ingredients:

- 1 cup dried chickpeas
- 4 cups water
- 1 tablespoon plus ¼ cup extra-virgin olive oil, divided
- ½ cup chopped roasted red pepper, divided
- 1/3 cup tahini
- 1 teaspoon ground cumin
- ¾ teaspoon salt
- ½ teaspoon ground black pepper
- ¼ teaspoon smoked paprika
- 1/3 cup lemon juice
- ½ teaspoon minced garlic

Direction:

1. Put chickpeas, water, and 1 tablespoon oil in the Instant Pot®. Seal, put steam release to Sealing, select Manual and time to 30 minutes.
2. When the timer rings, quick-release the pressure. Click Cancel button and open it. Drain, set aside the cooking liquid.
3. Process chickpeas, 1/3 cup roasted red pepper, remaining ¼ cup oil, tahini, cumin, salt, black pepper, paprika, lemon juice, and garlic using food processor. Serve, garnished with reserved roasted red pepper on top.

Nutrition: 96 Calories 8g Fat 2g Protein

16. White Bean Hummus

Preparation Time: 11 minutes
Cooking Time: 40 minutes
Serving: 12
Ingredients:

- 2/3 cup dried white beans
- 3 cloves garlic, peeled and crushed
- ¼ cup olive oil
- 1 tablespoon lemon juice
- ½ teaspoon salt

Direction

1. Place beans and garlic in the Instant Pot® and stir well. Add enough cold water to cover ingredients. Cover, set steam release to Sealing, select Manual button, and time to 30 minutes.
2. Once the timer stops, release pressure for 20 minutes. Select Cancel and open lid. Use a fork to check that beans are tender. Drain off excess water and transfer beans to a food processor.
3. Add oil, lemon juice, and salt to the processor and pulse until mixture is smooth with some small chunks. Pour into container and refrigerate for at least 4 hours. Serve cold or at room temperature.

Nutrition: 57 Calories 5g Fat 1g Protein

17. Kidney Bean Dip with Cilantro, Cumin, and Lime

Preparation Time: 13 minutes
Cooking Time: 51 minutes
Serving: 16
Ingredients:

- 1 cup dried kidney beans
- 4 cups water
- 3 cloves garlic
- ¼ cup cilantro
- ¼ cup extra-virgin olive oil
- 1 tablespoon lime juice
- 2 teaspoons grated lime zest
- 1 teaspoon ground cumin
- ½ teaspoon salt

Direction

1. Place beans, water, garlic, and 2 tablespoons cilantro in the Instant Pot®. Close the lid, select steam release to Sealing, click Bean button, and cook for 30 minutes.
2. When the timer alarms, let pressure release naturally, about 20 minutes. Press the Cancel button, open lid, and check that beans are tender. Drain off extra water and transfer beans to a medium bowl. Gently mash beans with potato masher. Add oil, lime juice, lime zest, cumin, salt, and remaining 2 tablespoons cilantro and stir to

combine. Serve warm or at room temperature.

Nutrition: 65 Calories 3g Fat 2g Protein

18.   White Bean Dip with Garlic and Herbs

Preparation Time: 10 minutes
Cooking Time: 48 minutes
Serving: 16
Ingredients:

- 1 cup dried white beans
- 3 cloves garlic
- 8 cups water
- ¼ cup extra-virgin olive oil
- ¼ cup chopped fresh flat-leaf parsley
- 1 tablespoon fresh oregano
- 1 tablespoon d fresh tarragon
- 1 teaspoon fresh thyme leaves
- 1 teaspoon lemon zest
- ¼ teaspoon salt
- ¼ teaspoon black pepper

Direction

1. Place beans and garlic in the Instant Pot® and stir well. Add water, close lid, put steam release to Sealing, press the Manual, and adjust time to 30 minutes.
2. When the timer beeps, release naturally, about 20 minutes. Open and check if beans are soft. Press the Cancel button, drain off excess water, and transfer beans and garlic to a food processor with olive oil. Add parsley, oregano, tarragon, thyme, lemon zest, salt, and pepper, and pulse 3–5 times to mix. Chill for 4 hours or overnight. Serve cold or at room temperature.

Nutrition: 47 Calories 3g Fat 1g Protein

19.   Black Bean Dip

Preparation Time: 14 minutes

Cooking Time: 53 minutes
Serving: 16
Ingredients:

- 1 tablespoon olive oil
- 2 slices bacon
- 1 small onion,
- 3 cloves garlic
- 1 cup low-sodium chicken broth
- 1 cup dried black beans
- 1 (14.5-ounce) can diced tomatoes
- 1 small jalapeño pepper
- 1 teaspoon ground cumin
- ½ teaspoon smoked paprika
- 1 tablespoon lime juice
- ½ teaspoon dried oregano
- ¼ cup minced fresh cilantro
- ¼ teaspoon sea salt

Direction:

1. Press the Sauté button on the Instant Pot® and heat oil. Add bacon and onion. Cook for 5 minutes. Cook garlic for 30 seconds. Fill in broth. Add beans, tomatoes, jalapeño, cumin, paprika, lime juice, oregano, cilantro, and salt. Press the Cancel button.
2. Close lid, let steam release to Sealing, set Bean button, and default time of 30 minutes. When the timer rings, let pressure release naturally for 10 minutes. Press the Cancel button and open lid.
3. Use an immersion blender blend the ingredients. Serve warm.

Nutrition: 60 Calories 2g Fat 3g Protein

20. Salsa Verde

Preparation Time: 9 minutes
Cooking Time: 21 minutes
Serving: 8
Ingredients:

- 1-pound tomatillos
- 2 small jalapeño peppers
- 1 small onion
- ½ cup chopped fresh cilantro
- 1 teaspoon ground coriander
- 1 teaspoon sea salt
- 1½ cups water

Direction:

1. Cut tomatillos in half and place in the Instant Pot®. Add enough water to cover.
2. Close lids, set steam release to Sealing, press the Manual button, and set time to 2 minutes. Once timer beeps, release pressure naturally, for 20 minutes. Press the Cancel and open lid.
3. Drain off excess water and transfer tomatillos to a food processor or blender, and add jalapeños, onion, cilantro, coriander, salt, and water. Pulse until well combined, about 20 pulses.
4. Wrap and cool for 2 hours before serving.

Nutrition: 27 Calories 1g Fat 1g Protein

21. Greek Eggplant Dip

Preparation Time: 16 minutes
Cooking Time: 3 minutes
Serving: 8
Ingredients:

- 1 cup water
- 1 large eggplant
- 1 clove garlic
- ½ teaspoon salt
- 1 tablespoon red wine vinegar
- ½ cup extra-virgin olive oil
- 2 tablespoons minced fresh parsley

Direction

1. Add water to the Instant Pot®, add the rack to the pot, and place the steamer basket on the rack.
2. Place eggplant in steamer basket. Close, set steam release to Sealing, turn on Manual button, and set time to 3 minutes. When the timer stops, quick-release the pressure. Click Cancel button and open.
3. Situate eggplant to a food processor and add garlic, salt, and vinegar. Pulse until smooth, about 20 pulses.
4. Slowly add oil to the eggplant mixture while the food processor runs continuously until oil is completely incorporated. Stir in parsley. Serve at room temperature.

Nutrition: 134 Calories 14g Fat 1g Protein

22. Baba Ghanoush

Preparation Time: 9 minutes
Cooking Time: 11 minutes
Serving: 8
Ingredients:

- 2 tablespoons extra-virgin olive oil
- 1 large eggplant
- 3 cloves garlic
- ½ cup water
- 3 tablespoons fresh flat-leaf parsley
- ½ teaspoon salt
- ¼ teaspoon smoked paprika
- 2 tablespoons lemon juice
- 2 tablespoons tahini

Direction

1. Press the Sauté button on the Instant Pot® and add 1 tablespoon oil. Add eggplant and cook until it begins to soften, about 5 minutes. Add garlic and cook 30 seconds.
2. Add water and close lid, click steam release to Sealing, select Manual, and time to 6 minutes. Once the timer rings, quick-release the pressure. Select Cancel and open lid.

3. Strain cooked eggplant and garlic and add to a food processor or blender along with parsley, salt, smoked paprika, lemon juice, and tahini. Add remaining 1 tablespoon oil and process. Serve warm or at room temperature.

Nutrition: 79 Calories 6g Fat 2g Protein

23. Chickpea, Parsley, and Dill Dip

Preparation Time: 11 minutes
Cooking Time: 22 minutes
Serving: 6
Ingredients:

- 8 cups water
- 1 cup dried chickpeas
- 3 tablespoons olive oil
- 2 garlic cloves
- 2 tablespoons fresh parsley
- 2 tablespoons fresh dill
- 1 tablespoon lemon juice
- ¼ teaspoon salt

Direction

1. Add 4 cups water and chickpeas to the Instant Pot®. Cover, place steam release to Sealing. Set Manual, and time to 1 minute. When the timer beeps, quick-release the pressure until the float valve drops, press the Cancel button, and open lid.
2. Drain water, rinse chickpeas, and return to pot with 4 cups fresh water. Set aside to soak for 1 hour.
3. Add 1 tablespoon oil to pot. Close, adjust steam release to Sealing, click Manual, and the time to 20 minutes. When alarm beeps, let pressure release for 20 minutes. Click the Cancel, open and drain chickpeas.
4. Place chickpeas to a food processor or blender, and add garlic, parsley, dill, lemon juice, and remaining 2 tablespoons water. Blend for about 30 seconds.
5. With the processor or blender lid still in place, slowly add

remaining 2 tablespoons oil while still blending, then add salt. Serve warm or at room temperature.

Nutrition 76 Calories 4g Fat 2g Protein

24. Instant Pot® Salsa

Preparation Time: 9 minutes
Cooking Time: 22 minutes
Serving: 12
Ingredients:

- 12 cups seeded diced tomatoes
- 6 ounces tomato paste
- 2 medium yellow onions
- 6 small jalapeño peppers
- 4 cloves garlic
- ¼ cup white vinegar
- ¼ cup lime juice
- 2 tablespoons granulated sugar
- 2 teaspoons salt
- ¼ cup chopped fresh cilantro

Direction:

1. Place tomatoes, tomato paste, onions, jalapeños, garlic, vinegar, lime juice, sugar, and salt in the Instant Pot® and stir well. Close it, situate steam release to Sealing. Click Manual button, and time to 20 minutes.
2. Once timer beeps, quick-release the pressure. Open, stir in cilantro, and press the Cancel button.
3. Let salsa cool to room temperature, about 40 minutes, then transfer to a storage container and refrigerate overnight.

Nutrition: 68 Calories 0.1g Fat 2g Protein

25. Sfougato

Preparation Time: 9 minutes
Cooking Time: 13 minutes

Serving: 4
Ingredients:

- ½ cup crumbled feta cheese
- ¼ cup bread crumbs
- 1 medium onion
- 4 tablespoons all-purpose flour
- 2 tablespoons fresh mint
- ½ teaspoon salt
- ½ teaspoon ground black pepper
- 1 tablespoon dried thyme
- 6 large eggs, beaten
- 1 cup water

Direction:

1. In a medium bowl, mix cheese, bread crumbs, onion, flour, mint, salt, pepper, and thyme. Stir in eggs.
2. Grease an 8" round baking dish with nonstick cooking spray. Pour egg mixture into dish.
3. Place rack in the Instant Pot® and add water. Crease a long piece of foil in half lengthwise. Lay foil over rack to form a sling and top with dish. Cover loosely with foil. Seal lid, put steam release in Sealing, select Manual, and time to 8 minutes.
4. When the timer alarms, release the pressure. Uncover. Let stand 5 minutes, then remove dish from pot.

Nutrition: 274 Calories 14g Fat 17g Protein

26. Skordalia

Preparation Time: 7 minutes
Cooking Time: 11 minutes
Serving: 16
Ingredients:

- 1-pound russet potatoes
- 3 cups plus ¼ cup water
- 2 teaspoons salt

- 8 cloves garlic
- ¾ cup blanched almonds
- ½ cup extra-virgin olive oil
- 2 tablespoons lemon juice
- 2 tablespoons white wine vinegar
- ½ teaspoon ground black pepper

Direction

1. Place potatoes, 3 cups water, and 1 teaspoon salt in the Instant Pot® and stir well. Close, set steam release to Sealing, click Manual button, and set to 10 minutes.
2. While potatoes cook, place garlic and remaining 1 teaspoon salt on a cutting board. With the side of a knife, press garlic and salt until it forms a paste. Transfer garlic paste into a food processor along with almonds and olive oil. Purée into a paste. Set aside.
3. When the timer beeps, quick-release the pressure. Select Cancel button and open lid. Strain potatoes then situate to a medium bowl. Add garlic mixture and mash with a potato masher until smooth. Stir in lemon juice, vinegar, and pepper. Stir in ¼ cup water a little at a time until mixture is thin enough for dipping. Serve warm or at room temperature.

Nutrition: 115 Calories 10g Fat 2g Protein

27. Pinto Bean Dip with Avocado Pico

Preparation Time: 6 minutes
Cooking Time: 52 minutes
Serving: 16
Ingredients:

- 1 cup dried pinto beans
- 4 cups water
- 4 tablespoons cilantro, divided
- 3 tablespoons extra-virgin olive oil
- 1 teaspoon ground cumin
- 1 clove garlic, peeled and minced
- ½ teaspoon salt

- 1 medium avocado
- 1 large ripe tomato
- 1 small jalapeño pepper
- ½ medium white onion
- 2 teaspoons lime juice

Direction

1. Place beans, water, and 2 tablespoons cilantro in the Instant Pot®. Close lid, place steam release to Sealing, click Bean and set default time of 30 minutes.
2. When the timer rings, let pressure release naturally. Open then check the beans are tender. Drain off excess water. Crush beans with fork. Add oil, cumin, garlic, and salt and mix well.
3. Toss remaining 2 tablespoons cilantro with avocado, tomato, jalapeño, onion, and lime juice. Spoon topping over bean dip. Serve.

Nutrition: 59 Calories 4g Fat 1g Protein

28. Power Pods & Hearty Hazelnuts with Mustard-y Mix

Preparation Time: 15 minutes
Cooking Time: 15 minutes
Serving: 4
Ingredients:

- 1-lb. green beans, trimmed
- 3-tbsp extra-virgin olive oil (divided)
- 2-tsp whole grain mustard
- 1-tbsp red wine vinegar
- ¼-tsp salt
- ¼-tsp ground pepper
- ¼-cup toasted hazelnuts, chopped

Directions:

1. Preheat your grill to high heat.
2. In a big mixing bowl, toss the green beans with a tablespoon of

olive oil. Place the beans in a grill basket. Grill for 8 minutes until charring a few spots, stirring occasionally.

3. Combine and whisk together the remaining oil, mustard, vinegar, salt, and pepper in the same mixing bowl. Add the grilled beans and toss to coat evenly.
4. To serve, top the side dish with hazelnuts.

Nutrition: 181 Calories 15g Fats 3g Protein

29. Peppery Potatoes

Preparation Time: 10 minutes
Cooking Time: 18 minutes
Serving: 4
Ingredients:

- 4-pcs large potatoes, cubed
- 4-tbsp extra-virgin olive oil (divided)
- 3-tbsp garlic, minced
- ½-cup coriander or cilantro, finely chopped
- 2-tbsp fresh lemon juice
- 1¾-tbsp paprika
- 2-tbsp parsley, minced

Directions:

1. Place the potatoes in a microwave-safe dish. Pour over a tablespoon of olive oil. Cover the dish tightly with plastic wrap. Heat the potatoes for seven minutes in your microwave to par-cook them.
2. Cook 2 tablespoons of olive oil in a pan placed over medium-low heat. Add the garlic and cover. Cook for 3 minutes. Add the coriander, and cook 2 minutes. Transfer the garlic-coriander sauce in a bowl, and set aside.
3. In the same pan placed over medium heat, heat 1 tablespoon of olive oil. Add the par-cooked potatoes. Do not stir! Cook for 3 minutes until browned, flipping once with a spatula. Continue cooking until browning all the sides.
4. Pull out the potatoes then situate them on a dish. Pour over the garlic-coriander sauce and lemon juice. Add the paprika, parsley,

and salt. Toss gently to coat evenly.

Nutrition: 316.2 Calories 14.2g Fats 4.5g Protein

30. Turkey Spheroids with Tzatziki Sauce

Preparation Time: 10 minutes
Cooking Time: 20 minutes
Serving: 8
Ingredients:
For Meatballs:

- 2-lbs ground turkey
- 2-tsp salt
- 2-cups zucchini, grated
- 1-tbsp lemon juice
- 1-cup crumbled feta cheese
- 1½-tsp pepper
- 1½-tsp garlic powder
- 1½-tbsp oregano
- ¼-cup red onion, finely minced

For Tzatziki Sauce:

- 1-tsp garlic powder
- 1-tsp dill
- 1-tbsp white vinegar
- 1-tbsp lemon juice
- 1-cup sour cream
- ½-cup grated cucumber
- Salt and pepper

Directions:

1. Preheat your oven to 350 °F.
2. For the Meatballs:
3. Incorporate all the meatball ingredients in a large mixing bowl. Mix well until fully combined. Form the turkey mixture into spheroids, using ¼-cup of the mixture per spheroid.
4. Heat a non-stick skillet placed over high heat. Add the meatballs,

and sear for 2 minutes.

5. Transfer the meatballs in a baking sheet. Situate the sheet in the oven, and bake for 15 minutes.
6. For the Tzatziki Sauce:
7. Combine and whisk together all the sauce ingredients in a medium-sized mixing bowl. Mix well until fully combined. Chill the sauce and serve.

Nutrition: 280 Calories 16g Fats 26.6g Protein

31. Greek Potato Skins with Olives and Feta

Preparation Time: 5 minutes
Cooking Time: 45 minutes
Servings: 4
Ingredients:

- 2 russet potatoes
- 3 tablespoons olive oil
- 1 teaspoon kosher salt, divided
- ¼ teaspoon black pepper
- 2 tablespoons fresh cilantro
- ¼ cup Kalamata olives, diced
- ¼ cup crumbled feta
- Chopped fresh parsley, for garnish (optional)

Directions:

1. Preheat the air fryer to 380°F. Using a fork, poke 2 to 3 holes in the potatoes, then coat each with about ½ tablespoon olive oil and ½ teaspoon salt.
2. Situate the potatoes into the air fryer basket and bake for 30 minutes. Remove the potatoes from the air fryer, and slice in half. Scrape out the flesh of the potatoes using a spoon, leaving a ½-inch layer of potato inside the skins, and set the skins aside.
3. In a medium bowl, combine the scooped potato middles with the remaining 2 tablespoons of olive oil, ½ teaspoon of salt, black pepper, and cilantro. Mix until well combined. Divide the potato filling into the now-empty potato skins, spreading it evenly over them. Top each potato with a tablespoon each of the olives and feta.
4. Place the loaded potato skins back into the air fryer and bake for 15 minutes. Serve with additional chopped cilantro or parsley and a drizzle of olive oil, if desired.

Nutrition 270 Calories 13g Fat 34g Carbohydrates 5g Protein

32. Artichoke and Olive Pita Flatbread

Preparation Time: 5 minutes

Cooking Time: 10 minutes
Servings: 4
Ingredients:

- 2 whole wheat pitas
- 2 tablespoons olive oil, divided
- 2 garlic cloves, minced
- ¼ teaspoon salt
- ½ cup canned artichoke hearts, sliced
- ¼ cup Kalamata olives
- ¼ cup shredded Parmesan
- ¼ cup crumbled feta
- Chopped fresh parsley, for garnish (optional)

Directions:

1. Preheat the air fryer to 380°F. Brush each pita with 1 tablespoon olive oil, then sprinkle the minced garlic and salt over the top.
2. Distribute the artichoke hearts, olives, and cheeses evenly between the two pitas, and place both into the air fryer to bake for 10 minutes. Remove the pitas and cut them into 4 pieces each before serving. Sprinkle parsley over the top, if desired.

Nutrition 243 Calories 15g Fat 10g Carbohydrates 7g Protein

33. Mini Crab Cakes

Preparation Time: 10 minutes
Cooking Time: 10 minutes
Servings: 6
Ingredients:

- 8 ounces lump crab meat
- 2 tablespoons diced red bell pepper
- 1 scallion, white parts and green parts, diced
- 1 garlic clove, minced
- 1 tablespoon capers, minced
- 1 tablespoon nonfat plain Greek yogurt
- 1 egg, beaten

- ¼ cup whole wheat bread crumbs
- ¼ teaspoon salt
- 1 tablespoon olive oil
- 1 lemon, cut into wedges

Directions:

1. Preheat the air fryer to 360°F. In a medium bowl, mix the crab, bell pepper, scallion, garlic, and capers until combined. Add the yogurt and egg. Stir until incorporated. Mix in the bread crumbs and salt.
2. Portion this mixture into 6 equal parts and pat out into patties. Place the crab cakes inside the air fryer basket on single layer, separately. Grease the tops of each patty with a bit of olive oil. Bake for 10 minutes.
3. Pull out the crab cakes from the air fryer and serve with lemon wedges on the side.

Nutrition 87 Calories 4g Fat 6g Carbohydrates 9g Protein

34. Zucchini Feta Roulades

Preparation Time: 10 minutes
Cooking Time: 10 minutes
Servings: 6
Ingredients:

- ½ cup feta
- 1 garlic clove, minced
- 2 tablespoons fresh basil, minced
- 1 tablespoon capers, minced
- 1/8 teaspoon salt
- 1/8 teaspoon red pepper flakes
- 1 tablespoon lemon juice
- 2 medium zucchinis
- 12 toothpicks

Directions:

1. Preheat the air fryer to 360°F. (If using a grill attachment, make

sure it is inside the air fryer during preheating.) In a small bowl, mix the feta, garlic, basil, capers, salt, red pepper flakes, and lemon juice.

2. Slice the zucchini into 1/8-inch strips lengthwise. (Each zucchini should yield around 6 strips.) Spread 1 tablespoon of the cheese filling onto each slice of zucchini, then roll it up and locked it with a toothpick through the middle.

3. Place the zucchini roulades into the air fryer basket in a one layer, individually. Bake or grill in the air fryer for 10 minutes. Remove the zucchini roulades from the air fryer and gently remove the toothpicks before serving.

Nutrition 46 Calories 3g Fat 6g Carbohydrates 3g Protein

35. Garlic-Roasted Tomatoes and Olives

Preparation Time: 5 minutes
Cooking Time: 20 minutes
Servings: 6
Ingredients:

- 2 cups cherry tomatoes
- 4 garlic cloves, roughly chopped
- ½ red onion, roughly chopped
- 1 cup black olives
- 1 cup green olives
- 1 tablespoon fresh basil, minced
- 1 tablespoon fresh oregano, minced
- 2 tablespoons olive oil
- ¼ to ½ teaspoon salt

Directions:

1. Preheat the air fryer to 380°F. In a large bowl, incorporate all of the ingredients and toss together so that the tomatoes and olives are coated well with the olive oil and herbs.

2. Pour the mixture into the air fryer basket, and roast for 10 minutes. Stir the mixture well, then continue roasting for an additional 10 minutes. Remove from the air fryer, transfer to a serving bowl, and

enjoy.

Nutrition 109 Calories 10g Fat 5g Carbohydrates 1g Protein

36. Goat Cheese and Garlic Crostini

Preparation Time: 3 minutes
Cooking Time: 5 minutes
Servings: 4
Ingredients:

- 1 whole wheat baguette
- ¼ cup olive oil
- 2 garlic cloves, minced
- 4 ounces goat cheese
- 2 tablespoons fresh basil, minced

Directions:

1. Preheat the air fryer to 380°F. Cut the baguette into ½-inch-thick slices. In a small bowl, incorporate together the olive oil and garlic, then brush it over one side of each slice of bread.
2. Place the olive-oil-coated bread in a single layer in the air fryer basket and bake for 5 minutes. In the meantime, combine together the goat cheese and basil. Remove the toast from the air fryer, then spread a thin layer of the goat cheese mixture over on each piece and serve.

Nutrition 365 Calories 21g Fat 10g Carbohydrates 12g Protein

37. Rosemary-Roasted Red Potatoes

Preparation Time: 5 minutes
Cooking Time: 20 minutes
Servings: 6
Ingredients:

- 1-pound red potatoes, quartered
- ¼ cup olive oil
- ½ teaspoon kosher salt

- ¼ teaspoon black pepper
- 1 garlic clove, minced
- 4 rosemary sprigs

Directions:

1. Preheat the air fryer to 360°F.
2. In a large bowl, toss in the potatoes with the olive oil, salt, pepper, and garlic until well coated. Fill the air fryer basket with potatoes and top with the sprigs of rosemary.
3. Roast for 10 minutes, then stir or toss the potatoes and roast for 10 minutes more. Remove the rosemary sprigs and serve the potatoes. Season well.

Nutrition 133 Calories 9g Fat 5g Carbohydrates 1g Protein

38. Guaca Egg Scramble

Preparation Time: 8 minutes
Cooking Time: 15 minutes
Servings: 4
Ingredients

- 4 eggs, beaten
- 1 white onion, diced
- 1 tablespoon avocado oil
- 1 avocado, finely chopped
- ½ teaspoon chili flakes
- 1 oz Cheddar cheese, shredded
- ½ teaspoon salt
- 1 tablespoon fresh parsley

Directions:

1. Pour avocado oil in the skillet and bring it to boil. Then add diced onion and roast it until it is light brown. Meanwhile, mix up together chili flakes, beaten eggs, and salt.
2. Fill the egg mixture over the cooked onion and cook the mixture for 1 minute over the medium heat. After this, scramble the eggs well

with the help of the fork or spatula. Cook the eggs until they are solid but soft.

3. After this, add chopped avocado and shredded cheese. Stir the scramble well and transfer in the serving plates. Sprinkle the meal with fresh parsley.

Nutrition 236 Calories 20g Fat 4g Carbohydrates 8.6g Protein

39. Morning Tostadas

Preparation Time: 15 minutes
Cooking Time: 6 minutes
Servings: 6
Ingredients

- ½ white onion, diced
- 1 tomato, chopped
- 1 cucumber, chopped
- 1 tablespoon fresh cilantro, chopped
- ½ jalapeno pepper, chopped
- 1 tablespoon lime juice
- 6 corn tortillas
- 1 tablespoon canola oil
- 2 oz Cheddar cheese, shredded
- ½ cup white beans, canned, drained
- 6 eggs
- ½ teaspoon butter
- ½ teaspoon Sea salt

Directions

1. Make Pico de Galo: in the salad bowl combine together diced white onion, tomato, cucumber, fresh cilantro, and jalapeno pepper. Then add lime juice and a ½ tablespoon of canola oil. Mix up the mixture well. Pico de Galo is cooked.
2. After this, preheat the oven to 390F. Line the tray with baking paper. Arrange the corn tortillas on the baking paper and brush with remaining canola oil from both sides. Bake the tortillas until they start to be crunchy. Chill the cooked crunchy tortillas well.

Meanwhile, toss the butter in the skillet.

3. Crack the eggs in the melted butter and sprinkle them with sea salt. Fry the eggs until the egg whites become white (cooked). Approximately for 3-5 minutes over the medium heat. After this, mash the beans until you get puree texture. Spread the bean puree on the corn tortillas.

4. Add fried eggs. Then top the eggs with Pico de Galo and shredded Cheddar cheese.

Nutrition 246 Calories 11g Fat 4.7g Carbohydrates 13.7g Protein

40. Cheese Omelet

Preparation Time: 5 minutes
Cooking Time: 10 minutes
Servings: 2
Ingredients

- 1 tablespoon cream cheese
- 2 eggs, beaten
- ¼ teaspoon paprika
- ½ teaspoon dried oregano
- ¼ teaspoon dried dill
- 1 oz Parmesan, grated
- 1 teaspoon coconut oil

Directions

1. Mix up together cream cheese with eggs, dried oregano, and dill. Pour coconut oil in the skillet and heat it up until it will coat all the skillet.

2. Then fill the skillet with the egg mixture and flatten it. Add grated Parmesan and close the lid. Cook omelet for 10 minutes over the low heat. Then transfer the cooked omelet in the serving plate and sprinkle with paprika.

Nutrition 148 Calories 11.5g Fat 0.3g Carbohydrates 10.6g Protein

41. Fruity Pizza

Preparation Time: 10 minutes
Cooking Time: 0 minute
Servings: 2
Ingredients

- 9 oz watermelon slice
- 1 tablespoon Pomegranate sauce
- 2 oz Feta cheese, crumbled
- 1 tablespoon fresh cilantro, chopped

Directions

1. Place the watermelon slice in the plate and sprinkle with crumbled Feta cheese. Add fresh cilantro. After this, sprinkle the pizza with Pomegranate juice generously. Cut the pizza into the servings.

Nutrition 143 Calories 6.2g Fat 0.6g Carbohydrates 5.1g Protein

42. Herb and Ham Muffins

Preparation Time: 10 minutes
Cooking Time: 15 minutes
Servings: 4
Ingredients

- 3 oz ham, chopped
- 4 eggs, beaten
- 2 tablespoons coconut flour
- ½ teaspoon dried oregano
- ¼ teaspoon dried cilantro
- Cooking spray

Directions

1. Spray the muffin's molds with cooking spray from inside. In the bowl mix up together beaten eggs, coconut flour, dried oregano, cilantro, and ham. When the liquid is homogenous, pour it in the prepared muffin molds.
2. Bake the muffins for 15 minutes at 360F. Chill the cooked meal

well and only after this remove from the molds.

Nutrition 128 Calories 7.2g Fat 2.9g Carbohydrates 10.1g Protein

43. Morning Sprouts Pizza

Preparation Time: 15 minutes
Cooking Time: 20 minutes
Servings: 6
Ingredients

- ½ cup wheat flour, whole grain
- 2 tablespoons butter, softened
- ¼ teaspoon baking powder
- ¾ teaspoon salt
- 5 oz chicken fillet, boiled
- 2 oz Cheddar cheese, shredded
- 1 teaspoon tomato sauce
- 1 oz bean sprouts

Directions

1. Make the pizza crust: mix up together wheat flour, butter, baking powder, and salt. Knead the soft and non-sticky dough. Add more wheat flour if needed. Leave the dough for 10 minutes to chill. Then place the dough on the baking paper. Cover it with the second baking paper sheet.
2. Roll up the dough with the help of the rolling pin to get the round pizza crust. After this, remove the upper baking paper sheet. Transfer the pizza crust in the tray.
3. Spread the crust with tomato sauce. Then shred the chicken fillet and arrange it over the pizza crust. Add shredded Cheddar cheese. Bake pizza for 20 minutes at 355F. Then top the cooked pizza with bean sprouts and slice into the servings.

Nutrition 157 Calories 8.8g Fat 0.3g Carbohydrates 10.5g Protein

44. Quinoa with Banana and Cinnamon

Preparation Time: 10 minutes

Cooking Time: 12 minutes
Servings: 4
Ingredients

- 1 cup quinoa
- 2 cup milk
- 1 teaspoon vanilla extract
- 1 teaspoon honey
- 2 bananas, sliced
- ¼ teaspoon ground cinnamon

Directions

1. Pour milk in the saucepan and add quinoa. Close the lid and cook it over the medium heat for 12 minutes or until quinoa will absorb all liquid. Then chill the quinoa for 10-15 minutes and place in the serving mason jars.
2. Add honey, vanilla extract, and ground cinnamon. Stir well. Top quinoa with banana and stirs it before serving.

Nutrition 279 Calories 5.3g Fat 4.6g Carbohydrates 10.7g Protein

45. Egg Casserole

Preparation Time: 10 minutes
Cooking Time: 28 minutes
Servings: 4
Ingredients

- 2 eggs, beaten
- 1 red bell pepper, chopped
- 1 chili pepper, chopped
- ½ red onion, diced
- 1 teaspoon canola oil
- ½ teaspoon salt
- 1 teaspoon paprika
- 1 tablespoon fresh cilantro, chopped
- 1 garlic clove, diced
- 1 teaspoon butter, softened

- ¼ teaspoon chili flakes

Directions

1. Brush the casserole mold with canola oil and pour beaten eggs inside. After this, toss the butter in the skillet and melt it over the medium heat. Add chili pepper and red bell pepper.
2. After this, add red onion and cook the vegetables for 7-8 minutes over the medium heat. Stir them from time to time. Transfer the vegetables in the casserole mold.
3. Add salt, paprika, cilantro, diced garlic, and chili flakes. Stir mildly with the help of a spatula to get a homogenous mixture. Bake the casserole for 20 minutes at 355F in the oven. Then chill the meal well and cut into servings. Transfer the casserole in the serving plates with the help of the spatula.

Nutrition 68 Calories 4.5g Fat 1g Carbohydrates 3.4g Protein

46. Cheese-Cauliflower Fritters

Preparation Time: 10 minutes
Cooking Time: 10 minutes
Servings: 2
Ingredients

- 1 cup cauliflower, shredded
- 1 egg, beaten
- 1 tablespoon wheat flour, whole grain
- 1 oz Parmesan, grated
- ½ teaspoon ground black pepper
- 1 tablespoon canola oil

Directions

1. In the mixing bowl mix up together shredded cauliflower and egg. Add wheat flour, grated Parmesan, and ground black pepper. Stir the mixture with the help of the fork until it is homogenous and smooth.
2. Pour canola oil in the skillet and bring it to boil. Make the fritters

from the cauliflower mixture with the help of the fingertips or use spoon and transfer in the hot oil. Roast the fritters for 4 minutes from each side over the medium-low heat.

Nutrition 167 Calories 12.3g Fat 1.5g Carbohydrates 8.8g Protein

47. Creamy Oatmeal Figs

Preparation Time: 10 minutes
Cooking Time: 20 minutes
Servings: 5
Ingredients

- 2 cups oatmeal
- 1 ½ cup milk
- 1 tablespoon butter
- 3 figs, chopped
- 1 tablespoon honey

Directions

1. Pour milk in the saucepan. Add oatmeal and close the lid. Cook the oatmeal for 15 minutes over the medium-low heat. Then add chopped figs and honey.
2. Add butter and mix up the oatmeal well. Cook it for 5 minutes more. Close the lid and let the cooked breakfast rest for 10 minutes before serving.

Nutrition 222 Calories 6g Fat 4.4g Carbohydrates 7.1g Protein

48. Baked Cinnamon Oatmeal

Preparation Time: 10 minutes
Cooking Time: 25 minutes
Servings: 4
Ingredients

- 1 cup oatmeal
- 1/3 cup milk
- 1 pear, chopped

- 1 teaspoon vanilla extract
- 1 tablespoon Splenda
- 1 teaspoon butter
- ½ teaspoon ground cinnamon
- 1 egg, beaten

Directions

1. In the big bowl mix up together oatmeal, milk, egg, vanilla extract, Splenda, and ground cinnamon. Melt butter and add it in the oatmeal mixture. Then add chopped pear and stir it well.
2. Transfer the oatmeal mixture in the casserole mold and flatten gently. Cover it with the foil and secure edges. Bake the oatmeal for 25 minutes at 350F.

Nutrition 151 Calories 3.9g Fat 3.3g Carbohydrates 4.9g Protein

49. Chia and Nut Porridge

Preparation Time: 10 minutes
Cooking Time: 30 minutes
Servings: 4
Ingredients

- 3 cups organic almond milk
- 1/3 cup chia seeds, dried
- 1 teaspoon vanilla extract
- 1 tablespoon honey
- ¼ teaspoon ground cardamom

Directions

1. Pour almond milk in the saucepan and bring it to boil. Then chill the almond milk to the room temperature (or appx. For 10-15 minutes). Add vanilla extract, honey, and ground cardamom. Stir well. After this, add chia seeds and stir again. Close the lid and let chia seeds soak the liquid for 20-25 minutes. Transfer the cooked porridge into the serving ramekins.

Nutrition 150 Calories 7.3g Fat 6.1g Carbohydrates 3.7g Protein

DINNER RECIPES

50. Chicken with Veggies

Preparation Time: 5 minutes
Cooking Time: 45 minutes
Servings: 4
Ingredients:

- 2 cups fingerling potatoes, halved
- 4 fresh figs, quartered
- 2 carrots, julienned
- 2 tablespoons extra-virgin olive oil
- 1 teaspoon sea salt, divided
- ¼ teaspoon freshly ground black pepper
- 4 chicken leg-thigh quarters
- 2 tablespoons chopped fresh parsley leaves

Directions:
1. Preheat the oven to 425°F. In a small bowl, toss the potatoes, figs, and carrots with the olive oil, ½ teaspoon of sea salt, and the pepper. Spread in a 9-by-13-inch baking dish.
2. Season the chicken with the rest of t sea salt. Place it on top of the vegetables. Bake until the internal temperature of 165°F. Sprinkle with the parsley and serve.

Nutrition 429 Calories 4g Fat 27g Carbohydrates 52g Protein

51. Tzatziki Chicken Gyros

Preparation Time: 15 minutes
Cooking Time: 80 minutes
Servings: 6
Ingredients:

- 1-pound ground chicken breast
- 1 onion, grated with excess water wrung out
- 2 tablespoons dried rosemary
- 1 tablespoon dried marjoram
-

6 garlic cloves, minced
- ½ teaspoon sea salt
- ¼ teaspoon freshly ground black pepper
- Tzatziki Sauce

Directions:

1. Preheat the oven to 350°F. Mix the chicken, onion, rosemary, marjoram, garlic, sea salt, and pepper using food processor. Blend until the mixture forms a paste. Alternatively, mix these ingredients in a bowl until well combined (see preparation tip).
2. Press the mixture into a loaf pan. Bake until it reaches 165 degrees internal temperature. Take out from the oven and let rest for 20 minutes before slicing.
3. Slice the gyro and spoon the tzatziki sauce over the top.

Nutrition 289 Calories 1g Fat 20g Carbohydrates 50g Protein

52. Greek Lasagna

Preparation Time: 10 minutes
Cooking Time: 45 minutes
Servings: 8

Ingredients:

- 5 tablespoons extra-virgin olive oil, divided
- 1 eggplant, sliced (unpeeled)
- 1 onion, chopped
- 1 green bell pepper, seeded and chopped
- 1-pound ground turkey
- 3 garlic cloves, minced
- 2 tablespoons tomato paste
- 1 (14-ounce) can chopped tomatoes, drained
- 1 tablespoon Italian seasoning
- 2 teaspoons Worcestershire sauce
- 1 teaspoon dried oregano
- ½ teaspoon ground cinnamon
- 1 cup unsweetened nonfat plain Greek yogurt
- 1 egg, beaten
- ¼ teaspoon freshly ground black pepper
- ¼ teaspoon ground nutmeg
- ¼ cup grated Parmesan cheese
- 2 tablespoons chopped fresh parsley leaves

Directions:

1. Preheat the oven to 400°F. Cook 3 tablespoons of olive oil until it shimmers. Add the eggplant slices and brown for 3 to 4 minutes per side. Transfer to paper towels to drain.
2. Situate the skillet back to the heat and pour the remaining 2 tablespoons of olive oil. Add the onion and green bell pepper. Continue cooking until the vegetables are soft. Remove from the pan and set aside.
3. Pull out the skillet to the heat and stir in the turkey. Cook for about 5 minutes, crumbling with a spoon, until browned. Cook garlic for 30 seconds, stirring constantly.
4. Stir in the tomato paste, tomatoes, Italian seasoning, Worcestershire

sauce, oregano, and cinnamon. Place the onion and bell pepper back to the pan. Cook for 5 minutes, stirring. Combine the yogurt, egg, pepper, nutmeg, and cheese.

5. Arrange half of the meat mixture in a 9-by-13-inch baking dish. Layer with half the eggplant. Add the remaining meat mixture and the remaining eggplant. Spread with the yogurt mixture. Bake until golden brown. Garnish with the parsley and serve.

Nutrition 338 Calories 5g Fat 16g Carbohydrates 28g Protein

53. Baked Pork Tenderloin

Preparation Time: 10 minutes
Cooking Time: 30 minutes
Servings: 6
Ingredients:

- ½ cup fresh Italian parsley leaves, chopped
- 3 tablespoons fresh rosemary leaves, chopped
- 3 tablespoons fresh thyme leaves, chopped
- 3 tablespoons Dijon mustard
- 1 tablespoon extra-virgin olive oil
- 4 garlic cloves, minced
- ½ teaspoon sea salt
- ¼ teaspoon freshly ground black pepper
- 1 (1½-pound) pork tenderloin

Directions:

1. Preheat the oven to 400°F. Blend the parsley, rosemary, thyme, mustard, olive oil, garlic, sea salt, and pepper. Process for about 30 seconds until smooth. Spread the mixture evenly over the pork and place it on a rimmed baking sheet.
2. Bake until the meat reaches an internal temperature of 140°F. Pull out from the oven and set aside for 10 minutes before slicing and serving.

Nutrition 393 Calories 3g Fat 5g Carbohydrates 74g Protein

54. Mushroom Sauce Steak

Preparation Time: 8 hours
Cooking Time: 20 minutes
Servings: 4
Ingredients:
For the Marinade and Steak

- 1 cup dry red wine
- 3 garlic cloves, minced
- 2 tablespoons extra-virgin olive oil
- 1 tablespoon low-sodium soy sauce
- 1 tablespoon dried thyme
- 1 teaspoon Dijon mustard
- 2 tablespoons extra-virgin olive oil
- 1 to 1½ pounds skirt steak, flat iron steak, or tri-tip steak

For the Mushroom Sauce

- 2 tablespoons extra-virgin olive oil
- 1-pound cremini mushrooms, quartered
- ½ teaspoon sea salt
- 1 teaspoon dried thyme
- 1/8 teaspoon freshly ground black pepper
- 2 garlic cloves, minced
- 1 cup dry red wine

Directions:
To Make the Marinade and Steak

1. In a small bowl, whisk the wine, garlic, olive oil, soy sauce, thyme, and mustard. Pour into a resealable bag and add the steak. Refrigerate the steak to marinate for 4 to 8 hours. Remove the steak from the marinade and pat it dry with paper towels.
2. Cook the olive oil in large pan until it shimmers.
3. Situate the steak and cook for about 4 minutes per side until deeply browned on each side and the steak reaches an internal temperature of 140°F. Remove the steak from the skillet and put it on a plate

tented with aluminum foil to keep warm, while you prepare the mushroom sauce.

4. When the mushroom sauce is ready, slice the steak against the grain into ½-inch-thick slices.

To Make the Mushroom Sauce

5. Cook oil in the same skillet over medium-high heat. Add the mushrooms, sea salt, thyme, and pepper. Cook for about 6 minutes, stirring very infrequently, until the mushrooms are browned.

6. Sauté the garlic. Mix in the wine. Cook until the liquid reduces by half. Serve the mushrooms spooned over the steak.

Nutrition 405 Calories 5g Fat 7g Carbohydrates 33g Protein

55. Keftedes

Preparation Time: 20 minutes
Cooking Time: 25 minutes
Servings: 4
Ingredients:

- 2 whole-wheat bread slices
- 1¼ pounds ground turkey
- 1 egg
- ¼ cup seasoned whole-wheat bread crumbs
- 3 garlic cloves, minced
- ¼ red onion, grated
- ¼ cup chopped fresh Italian parsley leaves
- 2 tablespoons chopped fresh mint leaves
- 2 tablespoons chopped fresh oregano leaves
- ½ teaspoon sea salt
- ¼ teaspoon freshly ground black pepper

Directions:

1. Preheat the oven to 350°F. Situate parchment paper or aluminum foil onto the baking sheet. Run the bread under water to wet it, and squeeze out any excess. Shred wet bread into small pieces and

place it in a medium bowl.

2. Add the turkey, egg, bread crumbs, garlic, red onion, parsley, mint, oregano, sea salt, and pepper. Mix well. Form the mixture into ¼-cup-size balls. Place the meatballs on the prepared sheet and bake for about 25 minutes, or until the internal temperature reaches 165°F.

Nutrition 350 Calories 6g Fat 10g Carbohydrates 42g Protein

56. String Beans and Tomatoes Lamb Chops

Preparation Time: 10 minutes
Cooking Time: 1 hour
Servings: 6
Ingredients:

- ¼ cup extra-virgin olive oil, divided
- 6 lamb chops, trimmed of extra fat
- 1 teaspoon sea salt, divided
- ½ teaspoon freshly ground black pepper
- 2 tablespoons tomato paste
- 1½ cups hot water
- 1-pound green beans, trimmed and halved crosswise
- 1 onion, chopped
- 2 tomatoes, chopped

Directions:

1. Cook 2 tablespoons of olive oil in large skillet until it shimmers. Season the lamb chops with ½ teaspoon of sea salt and 1/8 teaspoon of pepper. Cook the lamb in the hot oil for about 4 minutes per side until browned on both sides. Situate the meat to a platter and set aside.
2. Position the skillet back to the heat and put the remaining 2 tablespoons of olive oil. Heat until it shimmers.
3. In a bowl, melt the tomato paste in the hot water. Mix it to the hot skillet along with the green beans, onion, tomatoes, and the remaining ½ teaspoon of sea salt and ¼ teaspoon of pepper. Bring to a simmer, using the side of a spoon to scrape browned bits from

the bottom of the pan.

4. Return the lamb chops to the pan. Allow to boil and adjust the heat to medium-low. Simmer for 45 minutes until the beans are soft, adding additional water as needed to adjust the thickness of the sauce.

Nutrition 439 Calories 4g Fat 10g Carbohydrates 50g Protein

57. Chicken in Tomato-Balsamic Pan Sauce

Preparation Time: 10 minutes
Cooking Time: 20 minutes
Servings: 4
Ingredients

- 2 (8 oz. or 226.7 g each) boneless chicken breasts, skinless
- ½ tsp. salt
- ½ tsp. ground pepper
- 3 tbsps. extra-virgin olive oil
- ½ c. halved cherry tomatoes
- 2 tbsps. sliced shallot
- ¼ c. balsamic vinegar
- 1 tbsp. minced garlic
- 1 tbsp. toasted fennel seeds, crushed
- 1 tbsp. butter

Directions;

1. Slice the chicken breasts into 4 pieces and beat them with a mallet till it reaches a thickness of a ¼ inch. Use ¼ teaspoons of pepper and salt to coat the chicken. Heat two tablespoons of oil in a skillet and keep the heat to a medium. Cook the chicken breasts on each side for three minutes. Place it to a serving plate and cover it with foil to keep it warm.
2. Add one tablespoon oil, shallot, and tomatoes in a pan and cook till it softens. Add vinegar and boil the mix till the vinegar gets reduced by half. Put fennel seeds, garlic, salt, and pepper and cook for about four minutes. Pull it out from the heat and stir it with butter. Pour this sauce over chicken and serve.

Nutrition 294 Calories 17g Fat 10g Carbohydrates 2g Protein

58. Brown Rice, Feta, Fresh Pea, and Mint Salad

Preparation Time: 10 minutes
Cooking Time: 25 minutes
Servings: 4
Ingredients

- 2 c. brown rice
- 3 c. water
- Salt
- 5 oz. or 141.7 g crumbled feta cheese
- 2 c. cooked peas
- ½ c. chopped mint, fresh
- 2 tbsps. olive oil
- Salt and pepper

Directions:

1. Place the brown rice, water, and salt into a saucepan over medium heat, cover, and bring to boiling point. Turn the lower heat and allow it to cook until the water has dissolved and the rice is soft but chewy. Leave to cool completely
2. Add the feta, peas, mint, olive oil, salt, and pepper to a salad bowl with the cooled rice and toss to combine Serve and enjoy!

Nutrition 613 Calories 18.2g Fat 45g Carbohydrates 12g Protein

59. Whole Grain Pita Bread Stuffed with Olives and Chickpeas

Preparation Time: 10 minutes
Cooking Time 20 minutes
Servings: 2
Ingredients

- 2 wholegrain pita pockets
- 2 tbsps. olive oil

- 2 garlic cloves, chopped
- 1 onion, chopped
- ½ tsp. cumin
- 10 black olives, chopped
- 2 c. cooked chickpeas
- Salt and pepper

Directions:

1. Slice open the pita pockets and set aside Adjust your heat to medium and set a pan in place. Add in the olive oil and heat. Mix in the garlic, onion, and cumin to the hot pan and stir as the onions soften and the cumin is fragrant Add the olives, chickpeas, salt, and pepper and toss everything together until the chickpeas become golden
2. Set the pan from heat and use your wooden spoon to roughly mash the chickpeas so that some are intact and some are crushed Heat your pita pockets in the microwave, in the oven, or on a clean pan on the stove
3. Fill them with your chickpea mixture and enjoy!

Nutrition 503 Calories 19g Fat 14g Carbohydrates 15.7g Protein

60. Roasted Carrots with Walnuts and Cannellini Beans

Preparation Time: 10 minutes
Cooking Time: 45 minutes
Servings: 4
Ingredients

- 4 peeled carrots, chopped
- 1 c. walnuts
- 1 tbsp. honey
- 2 tbsps. olive oil
- 2 c. canned cannellini beans, drained
- 1 fresh thyme sprig
- Salt and pepper

Directions:

1. Set oven to 400 F/204 C and line a baking tray or roasting pan with baking paper Lay the carrots and walnuts onto the lined tray or pan Sprinkle olive oil and honey over the carrots and walnuts and give everything a rub to make sure each piece is coated Scatter the beans onto the tray and nestle into the carrots and walnuts
2. Add the thyme and sprinkle everything with salt and pepper Set tray in your oven and roast for about 40 minutes.
3. Serve and enjoy

Nutrition 385 Calories 27g Fat 6g Carbohydrates 18g Protein

61. Seasoned Buttered Chicken

Preparation Time: 10 minutes
Cooking Time: 20 minutes
Servings: 4
Ingredients

- ½ c. Heavy Whipping Cream
- 1 tbsp. Salt
- ½ c. Bone Broth
- 1 tbsp. Pepper
- 4 tbsps. Butter
- 4 Chicken Breast Halves

Directions:

1. Place cooking pan on your oven over medium heat and add in one tablespoon of butter. Once the butter is warm and melted, place the chicken in and cook for five minutes on either side. At the end of this time, the chicken should be cooked through and golden; if it is, go ahead and place it on a plate.
2. Next, you are going to add the bone broth into the warm pan. Add heavy whipping cream, salt, and pepper. Then, leave the pan alone until your sauce begins to simmer. Allow this process to happen for five minutes to let the sauce thicken up.
3. Finally, you are going to add the rest of your butter and the chicken back into the pan. Be sure to use a spoon to place the sauce over your chicken and smother it completely. Serve

Nutrition 350 Calories 25g Fat 10g Carbohydrates 25g Protein

62. Double Cheesy Bacon Chicken

Preparation Time: 10 minutes
Cooking Time: 30 minutes
Servings: 4
Ingredients

- 4 oz. or 113 g. Cream Cheese
- 1 c. Cheddar Cheese
- 8 strips Bacon
- Sea salt
- Pepper
- 2 Garlic cloves, finely chopped
- Chicken Breast
- 1 tbsp. Bacon Grease or Butter

Directions:

1. Ready the oven to 400 F/204 C Slice the chicken breasts in half to make them thin
2. Season with salt, pepper, and garlic Grease a baking pan with butter and place chicken breasts into it. Add the cream cheese and cheddar cheese on top of the breasts
3. Add bacon slices as well Place the pan to the oven for 30 minutes Serve hot

Nutrition 610 Calories 32g Fat 3g Carbohydrates 38g Protein

63. Shrimps with Lemon and Pepper

Preparation Time: 10 minutes
Cooking Time: 10 minutes
Servings: 4
Ingredients

- 40 deveined shrimps, peeled
- 6 minced garlic cloves
- Salt and black pepper

- 3 tbsps. olive oil
- ¼ tsp. sweet paprika
- A pinch crushed red pepper flake
- ¼ tsp. grated lemon zest
- 3 tbsps. Sherry or another wine
- 1½ tbsps. sliced chives
- Juice of 1 lemon

Directions:

1. Adjust your heat to medium-high and set a pan in place.
2. Add oil and shrimp, sprinkle with pepper and salt and cook for 1 minute Add paprika, garlic and pepper flakes, stir and cook for 1 minute. Gently stir in sherry and allow to cook for an extra minute
3. Take shrimp off the heat, add chives and lemon zest, stir and transfer shrimp to plates. Add lemon juice all over and serve

Nutrition 140 Calories 1g Fat5g Carbohydrates 18g Protein

64. <u>Breaded and Spiced Halibut</u>

Preparation Time: 5 minutes
Cooking Time: 25 minutes
Servings: 4
Ingredients

- ¼ c. chopped fresh chives
- ¼ c. chopped fresh dill
- ¼ tsp. ground black pepper
- ¾ c. panko breadcrumbs
- 1 tbsp. extra-virgin olive oil
- 1 tsp. finely grated lemon zest
- 1 tsp. sea salt
- 1/3 c. chopped fresh parsley
- 4 (6 oz. or 170 g. each) halibut fillets

Directions:

1. In a medium bowl, mix olive oil and the rest ingredients except

halibut fillets and breadcrumbs

2. Place halibut fillets into the mixture and marinate for 30 minutes Preheat your oven to 400 F/204 C Set a foil to a baking sheet, grease with cooking spray Dip the fillets to the breadcrumbs and put to the baking sheet Cook in the oven for 20 minutes Serve hot

Nutrition 667 Calories 24.5g Fat 2g Carbohydrates 54.8g Protein

65. Curry Salmon with Mustard

Preparation Time: 10 minutes
Cooking Time: 20 minutes
Servings: 4
Ingredients

- ¼ tsp. ground red pepper or chili powder
- ¼ tsp. turmeric, ground
- ¼ tsp. salt
- 1 tsp. honey
- ¼ tsp. garlic powder
- 2 tsps. whole grain mustard
- 4 (6 oz. or 170 g. each) salmon fillets

Directions:

1. In a bowl mix mustard and the rest ingredients except salmon Prep the oven to 350 F. Rub baking dish with cooking spray. Place salmon on baking dish with skin side down and spread evenly mustard mixture on top of fillets Place into the oven and cook for 10-15 minutes or until flaky

Nutrition 324 Calories 18.9g Fat 1.3g Carbohydrates 34g Protein

66. Walnut-Rosemary Crusted Salmon

Preparation Time: 10 minutes
Cooking Time: 25 minutes
Servings: 4
Ingredients

- 1 lb. or 450 g. frozen skinless salmon fillet
- 2 tsps. Dijon mustard
- 1 clove garlic, minced
- ¼ tsp. lemon zest
- ½ tsp. honey
- ½ tsp. kosher salt
- 1 tsp. freshly chopped rosemary
- 3 tbsps. panko breadcrumbs
- ¼ tsp. crushed red pepper
- 3 tbsps. chopped walnuts
- 2 tsp. extra-virgin olive oil

Directions:

1. Prepare the oven to 420 F/215 C and use parchment paper to line a rimmed baking sheet. In a bowl combine mustard, lemon zest, garlic, lemon juice, honey, rosemary, crushed red pepper, and salt. In another bowl mix walnut, panko, and 1 tsp oil Place parchments paper on the baking sheet and lay the salmon on it
2. Spread mustard mixture on the fish, and top with the panko mixture. Spray the rest of olive oil lightly on the salmon. Bake for about 10 -12 minutes or until the salmon is being separated by a fork Serve hot

Nutrition 222 Calories 12g Fat 4g Carbohydrates 0.8g Protein

67. Quick Tomato Spaghetti

Preparation Time: 10 minutes
Cooking Time: 25 minutes
Servings: 4
Ingredients

- 8 oz. or 226.7g spaghetti
- 3 tbsps. olive oil
- 4 garlic cloves, sliced
- 1 jalapeno, sliced
- 2 c. cherry tomatoes
- Salt and pepper

- 1 tsp. balsamic vinegar
- ½ c. Parmesan, grated

Directions:

1. Boil a large pot of water on medium flame. Add a pinch of salt and bring to a boil then add the spaghetti. Allow cooking for 8 minutes. While the pasta cooks, heat the oil in a skillet and add the garlic and jalapeno. Cook for an extra 1 minute then stir in the tomatoes, pepper, and salt.
2. Cook for 5-7 minutes until the tomatoes' skins burst.
3. Add the vinegar and remove off heat. Drain spaghetti well and mix it with the tomato sauce. Sprinkle with cheese and serve right away.

Nutrition 298 Calories 13.5g Fat 10.5g Carbohydrates 8g Protein

68. Chili Oregano Baked Cheese

Preparation Time: 10 minutes
Cooking Time: 25 minutes
Servings: 4
Ingredients

- 8 oz. or 226.7g feta cheese
- 4 oz. or 113g mozzarella, crumbled
- 1 sliced chili pepper
- 1 tsp. dried oregano
- 2 tbsps. olive oil

Directions:

1. Place the feta cheese in a small deep-dish baking pan. Top with the mozzarella then season with pepper slices and oregano. cover your pan with lid. Bake in the prepared oven at 350 F/176 C for 20 minutes. Serve the cheese and enjoy it.

Nutrition 292 Calories 24.2g Fat 5.7g Carbohydrates 2g Protein

69. Crispy Italian Chicken

Preparation Time: 10 minutes
Cooking Time: 30 minutes
Servings: 4
Ingredients

- 4 chicken legs
- 1 tsp. dried basil
- 1 tsp. dried oregano
- Salt and pepper
- 3 tbsps. olive oil
- 1 tbsp. balsamic vinegar

Directions:

1. Season the chicken well with basil, and oregano. Using a skillet, add oil and heat. Add the chicken in the hot oil. Let each side cook for 5 minutes until golden then cover the skillet with a lid.
2. Adjust your heat to medium and cook for 10 minutes on one side then flip the chicken repeatedly, cooking for another 10 minutes until crispy. Serve the chicken and enjoy.

Nutrition 262 Calories 13.9g Fat 11g Carbohydrates 32.6g Protein

70. Sea Bass in a Pocket

Preparation Time: 10 minutes
Cooking Time: 25 minutes
Servings: 4
Ingredients

- 4 sea bass fillets
- 4 sliced garlic cloves
- 1 sliced celery stalk
- 1 sliced zucchini
- 1 c. halved cherry tomatoes halved
- 1 shallot, sliced
- 1 tsp. dried oregano

- Salt and pepper

Directions:

1. Mix the garlic, celery, zucchini, tomatoes, shallot, and oregano in a bowl. Add salt and pepper to taste. Take 4 sheets of baking paper and arrange them on your working surface. Spoon the vegetable mixture in the center of each sheet.
2. Top with a fish fillet then wrap the paper well so it resembles a pocket. Place the wrapped fish in a baking tray and cook in the preheated oven at 350 F/176 C for 15 minutes. Serve the fish warm and fresh.

Nutrition 149 Calories 2.8g Fat 5.2g Carbohydrates 25.2g Protein

71. Creamy Smoked Salmon Pasta

Preparation Time: 5 minutes
Cooking Time: 35 minutes
Servings: 4
Ingredients

- 2 tbsps. olive oil
- 2 chopped garlic cloves
- 1 shallot, chopped
- 4 oz. or 113 g chopped salmon, smoked
- 1 c. green peas
- 1 c. heavy cream
- Salt and pepper
- 1 pinch chili flakes
- 8 oz. or 230 g penne pasta
- 6 c. water

Directions:

1. Place skillet on medium-high heat and add oil. Add the garlic and shallot. Cook for 5 minutes or until softened. Add peas, salt, pepper, and chili flakes. Cook for 10 minutes
2. Add the salmon, and continue cooking for 5-7 minutes more. Add

heavy cream, reduce heat and cook for an extra 5 minutes.

3. In the meantime, place a pan with water and salt to your taste on high heat as soon as it boils, add penne pasta and cook for 8-10 minutes or until softened Drain the pasta, add to the salmon sauce and serve

Nutrition 393 Calories 20.8g Fat 38g Carbohydrates 3g Protein

72. Slow Cooker Greek Chicken

Preparation Time 20 minutes
Cooking Time: 3 hours
Servings: 4
Ingredients

- 1 tablespoon extra-virgin olive oil
- 2 pounds boneless, chicken breasts
- ½ tsp kosher salt
- ¼ tsp black pepper
- 1 (12-ounce) jar roasted red peppers
- 1 cup Kalamata olives
- 1 medium red onion, cut into chunks
- 3 tablespoons red wine vinegar
- 1 tablespoon minced garlic
- 1 teaspoon honey
- 1 teaspoon dried oregano
- 1 teaspoon dried thyme
- ½ cup feta cheese (optional, for serving)

Directions

1. Brush slow cooker with nonstick cooking spray or olive oil. Cook the olive oil in a large skillet. Season both side of the chicken breasts. Once hot, stir in chicken breasts and sear on both sides (about 3 minutes).
2. Once cooked, transfer it to the slow cooker. Add the red peppers, olives, and red onion to the chicken breasts. Try to place the vegetables around the chicken and not directly on top.
3. In a small bowl, mix together the vinegar, garlic, honey, oregano,

and thyme. Once combined, pour it over the chicken. Cook the chicken on low for 3 hours or until no longer pink in the middle. Serve with crumbled feta cheese and fresh herbs.

Nutrition 399 Calories 17g Fat 12g Carbohydrates 50g Protein

73. Chicken Gyros

Preparation Time 10 minutes
Cooking Time: 4 hours
Servings: 4
Ingredients

- 2 lbs. boneless chicken breasts or chicken tenders
- Juice of one lemon
- 3 cloves garlic
- 2 teaspoons red wine vinegar
- 2–3 tablespoons olive oil
- ½ cup Greek yogurt
- 2 teaspoons dried oregano
- 2–4 teaspoons Greek seasoning
- ½ small red onion, chopped
- 2 tablespoons dill weed
- Tzatziki Sauce
- 1 cup plain Greek yogurt
- 1 tablespoon dill weed
- 1 small English cucumber, chopped
- Pinch of salt and pepper
- 1 teaspoon onion powder

Directions

1. Slice the chicken breasts into cubes and place in the slow cooker. Add the lemon juice, garlic, vinegar, olive oil, Greek yogurt, oregano, Greek seasoning, red onion, and dill to the slow cooker and stir to make sure everything is well combined.
2. Cook on low for 5–6 hours or on high for 2–3 hours. In the meantime, incorporate all ingredients for the tzatziki sauce and stir. When well mixed, put in the refrigerator until the chicken is done.

3. When the chicken has finished cooking, serve with pita bread and any or all of the toppings listed above.

Nutrition 317 Calories 7.4g Fat 36.1g Carbohydrates 28.6g Protein

74. Slow Cooker Chicken Cassoulet

Preparation Time: 10 minutes
Cooking Time: 20 minutes
Servings: 16
Ingredients

- 1 cup dry navy beans, soaked
- 8 bone-in skinless chicken thighs
- 1 Polish sausage, cooked and chopped into bite-sized pieces (optional)
- 1¼ cup tomato juice
- 1 (28-ounce) can halved tomatoes
- 1 tbsp Worcestershire sauce
- 1 tsp instant chicken bouillon granules
- ½ tsp dried basil
- ½ teaspoon dried oregano
- ½ teaspoon paprika
- ½ cup chopped celery
- ½ cup chopped carrot
- ½ cup chopped onion

Directions

1. Brush the slow cooker with olive oil or nonstick cooking spray. In a mixing bowl, stir together the tomato juice, tomatoes, Worcestershire sauce, beef bouillon, basil, oregano, and paprika. Make sure the ingredients are well combined.
2. Place the chicken and sausage into the slow cooker and cover with the tomato juice mixture. Top with celery, carrot, and onion. Cook on low for 10–12 hours.

Nutrition 244 Calories 7g Fat 25g Carbohydrates 21g Protein

75. Slow Cooker Chicken Provencal

Preparation Time 5 minutes
Cooking Time: 8 hours
Servings: 4
Ingredients

- 4 (6-ounce) skinless bone-in chicken breast halves
- 2 teaspoons dried basil
- 1 teaspoon dried thyme
- 1/8 teaspoon salt
- 1/8 teaspoon freshly ground black pepper
- 1 yellow pepper, diced
- 1 red pepper, diced
- 1 (15.5-ounce) can cannellini beans
- 1 (14.5-ounce) can petite tomatoes with basil, garlic, and oregano, undrained

Directions

1. Brush the slow cooker with nonstick olive oil. Add all the ingredients to the slow cooker and stir to combine. Cook on low for 8 hours.

Nutrition 304 Calories 4.5g Fat 27.3g Carbohydrates 39.4g Protein

76. Greek Style Turkey Roast

Preparation Time: 20 minutes
Cooking Time: 7 hours and 30 minutes
Servings: 8
Ingredients

- 1 (4-pound) boneless turkey breast, trimmed
- ½ cup chicken broth, divided
- 2 tablespoons fresh lemon juice
- 2 cups chopped onion
- ½ cup pitted Kalamata olives
- ½ cup oil-packed sun-dried tomatoes, thinly sliced

- 1 teaspoon Greek seasoning
- ½ teaspoon salt
- ¼ teaspoon fresh ground black pepper
- 3 tablespoons all-purpose flour (or whole wheat)

Directions

1. Brush the slow cooker with nonstick cooking spray or olive oil. Add the turkey, ¼ cup of the chicken broth, lemon juice, onion, olives, sun-dried tomatoes, Greek seasoning, salt and pepper to the slow cooker.
2. Cook on low for 7 hours. Scourge the flour into the remaining ¼ cup of chicken broth, then stir gently into the slow cooker. Cook for an additional 30 minutes.

Nutrition 341 Calories 19g Fat 12g Carbohydrates 36.4g Protein

77. Garlic Chicken with Couscous

Preparation Time: 25 minutes
Cooking Time: 7 hours
Servings: 4
Ingredients

- 1 whole chicken, cut into pieces
- 1 tablespoon extra-virgin olive oil
- 6 cloves garlic, halved
- 1 cup dry white wine
- 1 cup couscous
- ½ teaspoon salt
- ½ teaspoon pepper
- 1 medium onion, thinly sliced
- 2 teaspoons dried thyme
- 1/3 cup whole wheat flour

Directions

1. Cook the olive oil in a heavy skillet. When skillet is hot, add the chicken to sear. Make sure the chicken pieces don't touch each

other. Cook with the skin side down for about 3 minutes or until browned.
2. Brush your slow cooker with nonstick cooking spray or olive oil. Put the onion, garlic, and thyme into the slow cooker and sprinkle with salt and pepper. Stir in the chicken on top of the onions.
3. In a separate bowl, whisk the flour into the wine until there are no lumps, then pour over the chicken. Cook at low for 7 hours. You can cook on high for 3 hours as well. Serve the chicken over the cooked couscous and spoon sauce over the top.

Nutrition 440 Calories 17.5g Fat 14g Carbohydrates 35.8g Protein

78. Chicken Karahi

Preparation Time: 5 minutes
Cooking Time: 5 hours
Servings: 4
Ingredients

- 2 lbs. chicken breasts or thighs
- ¼ cup olive oil
- 1 small can tomato paste
- 1 tablespoon butter
- 1 large onion, diced
- ½ cup plain Greek yogurt
- ½ cup water
- 2 tablespoons ginger in garlic paste
- 3 tablespoons fenugreek leaves
- 1 teaspoon ground coriander
- 1 medium tomato
- 1 teaspoon red chili
- 2 green chilies
- 1 teaspoon turmeric
- 1 tablespoon garam masala
- 1 teaspoon cumin powder
- 1 teaspoon sea salt
- ¼ teaspoon nutmeg

Directions

1. Brush the slow cooker with nonstick cooking spray. In a small bowl, thoroughly mix together all of the spices. Mix in the chicken to the slow cooker followed by the rest of the ingredients, including the spice mixture. Stir until everything is well mixed with the spices.
2. Cook on low for 4–5 hours. Serve with naan or Italian bread.

Nutrition 345 Calories 9.9g Fat 10g Carbohydrates 53.7g Protein

79. Chicken Cacciatore with Orzo

Preparation Time: 20 minutes
Cooking Time: 4 hours
Servings: 6
Ingredients

- 2 pounds skin-on chicken thighs
- 1 tablespoon olive oil
- 1 cup mushrooms, quartered
- 3 carrots, chopped
- 1 small jar Kalamata olives
- 2 (14-ounce) cans diced tomatoes
- 1 small can tomato paste
- 1 cup red wine
- 5 garlic cloves
- 1 cup orzo

Directions

1. In a large skillet, cook the olive oil. When the oil is heated, add the chicken, skin side down, and sear it.
2. When the chicken is browned, add to the slow cooker along with all the ingredients except the orzo. Cook the chicken at low for 2 hours, then add the orzo and cook for an additional 2 hours. Serve with a crusty French bread.

Nutrition 424 Calories 16g Fat 10g Carbohydrates 11g Protein

80. Slow Cooker Beef Daube

Preparation Time: 15 minutes
Cooking Time: 8 hours
Servings: 8

Ingredients

- 1 tablespoon olive oil
- 10 garlic cloves, minced
- 2 pounds boneless chuck roast
- 1½ teaspoons salt, divided
- ½ teaspoon freshly ground black pepper
- 1 cup dry red wine
- 2 cups carrots, chopped
- 1½ cups onion, chopped
- ½ cup beef broth
- 1 (14-ounce) can diced tomatoes
- 1 tablespoon tomato paste
- 1 teaspoon fresh rosemary, chopped
- 1 teaspoon fresh thyme, chopped
- ½ teaspoon orange zest, grated
- ½ teaspoon ground cinnamon
- ¼ teaspoon ground cloves
- 1 bay leaf

Directions

1. Preheat a skillet and then add the olive oil. Add the minced garlic and onions and cook until the onions are soft and the garlic begins to brown.
2. Add the cubed meat, salt, and pepper and cook until the meat has browned. Transfer the meat to the slow cooker. Mix in the beef broth to the skillet and let simmer for about 3 minutes to deglaze the pan, then pour into slow cooker over the meat.
3. Incorporate the rest of the ingredients to the slow cooker and stir well to combine. Adjust slow cooker to low and cook for 8 hours, or set to high and cook for 4 hours. Serve with a side of egg noodles, rice or some crusty Italian bread.

Nutrition 547 Calories 30.5g Fat 22g Carbohydrates 45.2g Protein

81. Slow-Cooked Veal Shanks

Preparation Time: 30 minutes
Cooking Time: 8 hours
Servings: 3
Ingredients

- 4 beef shanks or veal shanks
- 1 teaspoon sea salt
- ½ teaspoon ground black pepper
- 3 tablespoons whole wheat flour
- 1–2 tablespoons olive oil
- 2 medium onions, diced
- 2 medium carrots, diced
- 2 celery stalks, diced
- 4 garlic cloves, minced
- 1 (14-ounce) can diced tomatoes
- 2 teaspoons dried thyme leaves
- ½ cup beef or vegetable stock

Directions

1. Season the shanks on both sides, then dip in the flour to coat. Heat a large skillet over high heat. Add the olive oil. Once hot, situate shanks and brown evenly on both sides. When browned, transfer to the slow cooker.
2. Pour the stock into the skillet and let simmer for 3–5 minutes while stirring to deglaze the pan. Transfer the rest of the ingredients to the slow cooker and pour the stock from the skillet over the top.
3. Adjust the slow cooker to low and cook for 8 hours. Serve the Osso Bucco over quinoa, brown rice, or even cauliflower rice.

Nutrition 589 Calories 21.3g Fat 15g Carbohydrates 74.7g Protein

82. Crockpot Beef Bourguignon

Preparation Time: 5 minutes

Cooking Time: 8 hours
Servings: 8
Ingredients

- 1 tablespoon extra-virgin olive oil
- 6 ounces bacon, roughly chopped
- 3 pounds beef brisket, trimmed of fat, cut into 2-inch cubes
- 1 large carrot, sliced
- 1 large white onion, diced
- 6 cloves garlic, minced and divided
- ½ teaspoon coarse salt
- ½ teaspoon freshly ground pepper
- 2 tablespoons whole wheat
- 12 small pearl onions
- 3 cups red wine (Merlot, Pinot Noir, or Chianti)
- 2 cups beef stock
- 2 tablespoons tomato paste
- 1 beef bouillon cube, crushed
- 1 teaspoon fresh thyme, finely chopped
- 2 tablespoons fresh parsley
- 2 bay leaves
- 2 tablespoons butter or 1 tablespoon olive oil
- 1 pound fresh small white or brown mushrooms, quartered

Directions

1. Preheat skillet over medium-high heat, then add the olive oil. When the oil has heated, cook the bacon until it is crisp, then place it in your slow cooker. Save the bacon fat in the skillet.
2. Pat dry the beef and cook it in the same skillet with the bacon fat until all sides have the same brown coloring. Transfer to the slow cooker.
3. Mix in the onions and carrots to the slow cooker and season with the salt and pepper. Stir to combine the ingredients and make sure everything is seasoned.
4. Stir in the red wine into the skillet and simmer for 4–5 minutes to deglaze the pan, then whisk in the flour, stirring until smooth.

Continue cooking until the liquid reduces and thickens a bit.

5. When the liquid has thickened, pour it into the slow cooker and stir to coat everything with the wine mixture. Add the tomato paste, bouillon cube, thyme, parsley, 4 cloves of garlic, and bay leaf. Adjust your slow cooker to high and cook for 6 hours, or set to low and cook for 8 hours.

6. Soften the butter or heat the olive oil in a skillet over medium heat. When hot, stir in the remaining 2 cloves of garlic and cook for about 1 minute before adding the mushrooms. Cook the mushrooms until soft, then add to the slow cooker and mix to combine.

7. Serve with mashed potatoes, rice or noodles.

Nutrition 672 Calories 32g Fat 15g Carbohydrates 56g Protein

83. Balsamic Chuck Roast

Preparation Time: 5 minutes
Cooking Time: 8 hours
Servings: 10
Ingredients

- 2 pounds boneless chuck roast
- 1 tablespoon olive oil

Rub

- 1 teaspoon garlic powder
- ½ teaspoon onion powder
- 1 teaspoon sea salt
- ½ teaspoon freshly ground black pepper

Sauce

- ½ cup balsamic vinegar
- 2 tablespoons honey
- 1 tablespoon honey mustard
- 1 cup beef broth
- 1 tablespoon tapioca, whole wheat flour, or cornstarch (to thicken sauce when it is done cooking if desired)

Directions

1. Incorporate all of the ingredients for the rub.
2. In a separate bowl, mix the balsamic vinegar, honey, honey mustard, and beef broth. Coat the roast in olive oil, then rub in the spices from the rub mix. Situate roast in the slow cooker and then pour the sauce over the top. Adjust the slow cooker to low and cook for 8 hours.
3. If you want to thicken the sauce when the roast is done cooking transfer it from the slow cooker to a serving plate. Then fill the liquid into a saucepan and heat to boiling on the stovetop. Mix the flour until smooth and let simmer until the sauce thickens.

Nutrition 306 Calories 19g Fat 13g Carbohydrates 25g Protein

84. Pot-Roast Veal

Preparation Time: 20 minutes
Cooking Time: 5 hours
Servings: 8
Ingredients

- 2 tablespoons olive oil
- Salt and pepper
- 3-pound boneless veal roast, tied
- 4 medium carrots, peeled
- 2 parsnips, peeled and halved
- 2 white turnips, peeled and quartered
- 10 garlic cloves, peeled
- 2 sprigs fresh thyme
- 1 orange, scrubbed and zested
- 1 cup chicken or veal stock

Directions

1. Heat a large skillet over medium-high heat. Scour veal roast all over with olive oil, then season with salt and pepper. Once hot, situate the veal roast and sear on all sides. This will take about 3 minutes on every side, but this process seals in the juices and

makes the meat succulent.

2. When cooked, place it to the slow cooker. Throw in the carrots, parsnips, turnips, and garlic into the skillet. Cook for 5 minutes.
3. Situate vegetables to the slow cooker, placing them all around the meat. Top the roast with the thyme and the zest from the orange. Slice the orange into 2 and squeeze the juice over the top of the meat. Fill in chicken stock, then cook the roast on low for 5 hours.

Nutrition 421 Calories 12.8g Fat 10g Carbohydrates 48.8g Protein

85. Medi Sausage with Rice

Preparation Time: 15 minutes
Cooking Time 8 hours
Servings: 6
Ingredients

- 1½ pounds Italian sausage, crumbled
- 1 medium onion, chopped
- 2 tablespoons steak sauce
- 2 cups long grain rice, uncooked
- 1 (14-ounce) can diced tomatoes with juice
- ½ cup water
- 1 medium green pepper, diced

Directions

1. Spray your slow cooker with olive oil or nonstick cooking spray. Add the sausage, onion, and steak sauce to the slow cooker. Put on low for 9 hours.
2. After 8 hours, add the rice, tomatoes, water and green pepper. Stir to combine thoroughly. Cook an additional 20 to 25 minutes.

Nutrition 650 Calories 36g Fat 11g Carbohydrates 22g Protein

86. Albondigas

Preparation Time: 20 minutes
Cooking Time 5 hours
Servings: 6

Ingredients

- 1-pound ground turkey
- 1-pound ground pork
- 2 eggs
- 1 (20-ounce) can diced tomatoes
- ¾ cup sweet onion, minced, divided
- ¼ cup plus 1 tablespoon breadcrumbs
- 3 tablespoons fresh parsley, chopped
- 1½ teaspoons cumin
- 1½ teaspoons paprika (sweet or hot)

Directions

1. Spray the slow cooker with olive oil.
2. In a mixing bowl, incorporate the ground meat, eggs, about half of the onions, the breadcrumbs, and the spices.
3. Wash your hands and mix together until everything is well combined. Do not over-mix, though, as this makes for tough meatballs. Shape into meatballs. How big you make them will obviously determine how many total meatballs you get.
4. In a skillet, cook 2 tablespoons of olive oil over medium heat. Once hot, mix in the meatballs and brown on all sides. Make sure the balls aren't touching each other so they brown evenly. Once done, transfer them to the slow cooker.
5. Add the rest of the onions and the tomatoes to the skillet and allow them to cook for a few minutes, scraping the brown bits from the meatballs up to add flavor. Transfer the tomatoes over the meatballs in the slow cooker and cook on low for 5 hours.

Nutrition 372 Calories 21.7g Fat 15g Carbohydrates 28.6 Protein

87. Baked Bean Fish Meal

Preparation Time: 10 minutes
Cooking Time: 10 minutes
Servings: 4
Ingredients:

- 1 tablespoon balsamic vinegar
- 2 ½ cups green beans
- 1-pint cherry or grape tomatoes
- 4 (4-ounce each) fish fillets, such as cod or tilapia
- 2 tablespoons olive oil

Directions:

1. Preheat an oven to 400 degrees. Grease two baking sheets with some olive oil or olive oil spray. Arrange 2 fish fillets on each sheet. In a mixing bowl, pour olive oil and vinegar. Combine to mix well with each other.
2. Mix green beans and tomatoes. Combine to mix well with each other. Combine both mixtures well with each other. Add mixture equally over fish fillets. Bake for 6-8 minutes, until fish opaque and easy to flake. Serve warm.

Nutrition 229 Calories 13g Fat 2.5g Protein

88. Mushroom Cod Stew

Preparation Time: 10 minutes
Cooking Time: 20 minutes
Servings: 6
Ingredients:

- 2 tablespoons extra-virgin olive oil
- 2 garlic cloves, minced
- 1 can tomato
- 2 cups chopped onion
- ¾ teaspoon smoked paprika
- a (12-ounce) jar roasted red peppers
- 1/3 cup dry red wine
- ¼ teaspoon kosher or sea salt
- ¼ teaspoon black pepper
- 1 cup black olives
- 1 ½ pounds cod fillets, cut into 1-inch pieces
- 3 cups sliced mushrooms

Directions:

1. Get medium-large cooking pot, warm up oil over medium heat. Add onions and stir-cook for 4 minutes.
2. Add garlic and smoked paprika; cook for 1 minute, stirring often. Add tomatoes with juice, roasted peppers, olives, wine, pepper, and salt; stir gently.
3. Boil mixture. Add the cod and mushrooms; turn down heat to medium. Close and cook until the cod is easy to flake, stir in between. Serve warm.

Nutrition 238 Calories 7g Fat 3.5g Protein

89. Spiced Swordfish

Preparation Time: 10 minutes
Cooking Time: 15 minutes
Servings: 4
Ingredients:

- 4 (7 ounces each) swordfish steaks
- 1/2 teaspoon ground black pepper
- 12 cloves of garlic, peeled
- 3/4 teaspoon salt
- 1 1/2 teaspoon ground cumin
- 1 teaspoon paprika
- 1 teaspoon coriander
- 3 tablespoons lemon juice
- 1/3 cup olive oil

Directions:

1. Using food processor, incorporate all the ingredients excluding for swordfish. Secure the lid and blend until smooth mixture. Pat dry fish steaks; coat equally with the prepared spice mixture.
2. Situate them over an aluminum foil, cover and refrigerator for 1 hour. Prep a griddle pan over high heat, pour oil and heat it. Stir in fish steaks; stir-cook for 5-6 minutes per side. Serve warm.

Nutrition 255 Calories 12g Fat 0.5g Protein

90. Anchovy Pasta Mania

Preparation Time: 10 minutes
Cooking Time: 20 minutes
Servings: 4
Ingredients:

- 4 anchovy fillets, packed in olive oil
- ½ pound broccoli, cut into 1-inch florets
- 2 cloves garlic, sliced
- 1-pound whole-wheat penne
- 2 tablespoons olive oil
- ¼ cup Parmesan cheese, grated
- Salt and black pepper, to taste
- Red pepper flakes, to taste

Directions:

1. Cook pasta as directed over pack; drain and set aside. Take a medium saucepan or skillet, add oil. Heat over medium heat.
2. Add anchovies, broccoli, and garlic, and stir-cook until veggies turn tender for 4-5 minutes. Take off heat; mix in the pasta. Serve warm with Parmesan cheese, red pepper flakes, salt, and black pepper sprinkled on top.

Nutrition 328 Calories 8g Fat 7g Protein

91. Shrimp Garlic Pasta

Preparation Time: 10 minutes
Cooking Time: 15 minutes
Servings: 4
Ingredients:

- 1-pound shrimp
- 3 garlic cloves, minced
- 1 onion, finely chopped
- 1 package whole wheat or bean pasta
- 4 tablespoons olive oil

- Salt and black pepper, to taste
- ¼ cup basil, cut into strips
- ¾ cup chicken broth, low-sodium

Directions:

1. Cook pasta as directed over pack; rinse and set aside. Get medium saucepan, add oil then warm up over medium heat. Add onion, garlic and stir-cook until become translucent and fragrant for 3 minutes.
2. Add shrimp, black pepper (ground) and salt; stir-cook for 3 minutes until shrimps are opaque. Add broth and simmer for 2-3 more minutes. Add pasta in serving plates; add shrimp mixture over; serve warm with basil on top.

Nutrition 605 Calories 17g Fat 19g Protein

DESSERT RECIPES

92. Key Lime Pie

Preparation time: 15 minutes
Cooking Time: 8 minutes
Servings: 8
Ingredients

- 1 (9-inch) prepared graham cracker crust
- 3 cups of sweetened condensed milk
- 1/2 cup sour cream
- 3/4 cup lime juice
- 1 tablespoon grated lime zest

Direction

1. Prepare oven to 175 ° C
2. Combine the condensed milk, sour cream, lime juice, and lime zest in a medium bowl. Mix well and transfer into the graham cracker crust.
3. Bake in the preheated oven for 5 to 8 minutes
4. Cool the cake well before serving. Decorate with lime slices and

whipped cream if desired.

Nutrition: 553 calories 20.5g fat 10.9g protein

93. Rhubarb Strawberry Crunch

Preparation time: 15 minutes
Cooking Time: 45 minutes
Servings: 18
Ingredients

- 1 cup of white sugar
- 3 tablespoons all-purpose flour
- 3 cups of fresh strawberries, sliced
- 3 cups of rhubarb, cut into cubes
- 1 1/2 cup flour
- 1 cup packed brown sugar
- 1 cup butter
- 1 cup oatmeal

Direction

1. Preheat the oven to 190 ° C.
2. Incorporate white sugar, 3 tablespoons flour, strawberries and rhubarb in a large bowl. Place the mixture in a 9 x 13-inch baking dish.
3. Mix 1 1/2 cups of flour, brown sugar, butter, and oats until a crumbly texture is obtained. You may want to use a blender for this. Crumble the mixture of rhubarb and strawberry.
4. Bake for 45 minutes.

Nutrition: 253 calories 10.8g fat 2.3g protein

94. Chocolate Chip Banana Dessert

Preparation Time: 20 minutes
Cooking Time: 20 minutes
Servings: 24
Ingredients

- 2/3 cup white sugar
- 3/4 cup butter
- 2/3 cup brown sugar
- 1 egg, beaten slightly
- 1 teaspoon vanilla extract
- 1 cup of banana puree
- 1 3/4 cup flour
- 2 teaspoons baking powder
- 1/2 teaspoon of salt
- 1 cup of semi-sweet chocolate chips

Direction:

1. Ready the oven to 175 ° C Grease and bake a 10 x 15-inch baking pan.
2. Beat the butter, white sugar, and brown sugar in a large bowl until light. Beat the egg and vanilla. Fold in the banana puree: mix baking powder, flour, and salt in another bowl. Mix flour mixture into the butter mixture. Stir in the chocolate chips. Spread in pan.
3. Bake for 20 minutes. Cool before cutting into squares.

Nutrition: 174 calories 8.2g fat 1.7g protein

95. Apple Pie Filling

Preparation time: 20 minutes
Cooking Time: 12 minutes
Servings: 40
Ingredients

- 18 cups chopped apples
- 3 tablespoons lemon juice
- 10 cups of water
- 4 1/2 cups of white sugar
- 1 cup corn flour
- 2 teaspoons of ground cinnamon
- 1 teaspoon of salt
- 1/4 teaspoon ground nutmeg

Direction

1. Mix apples with lemon juice in a large bowl and set aside. Pour the water in a Dutch oven over medium heat. Combine sugar, corn flour, cinnamon, salt, and nutmeg in a bowl. Add to water, mix well, and bring to a boil. Cook for 2 minutes with continuous stirring.
2. Boil apples again. Reduce the heat, cover, and simmer for 8 minutes. Allow cooling for 30 minutes.
3. Pour into five freezer containers and leave 1/2 inch of free space. Cool to room temperature.
4. Seal and freeze

Nutrition: 129 calories 0.1g fat0.2g protein

96. Ice Cream Sandwich Dessert

Preparation Time: 20 minutes
Cooking Time: 0 minute
Servings: 12
Ingredients

- 22 ice cream sandwiches
- Frozen whipped topping in 16 oz container, thawed
- 1 jar (12 oz) Caramel ice cream
- 1 1/2 cups of salted peanuts

Direction

1. Cut a sandwich with ice in two. Place a whole sandwich and a half sandwich on a short side of a 9 x 13-inch baking dish. Repeat this until the bottom is covered, alternate the full sandwich, and the half sandwich.
2. Spread half of the whipped topping. Pour the caramel over it. Sprinkle with half the peanuts. Do layers with the rest of the ice cream sandwiches, whipped cream, and peanuts.
3. Cover and freeze for 2 months. Remove from the freezer 20 minutes before serving. Cut into squares.

Nutrition: 559 calories 28.8g fat 10g protein

97. Cranberry and Pistachio Biscotti

Preparation time: 15 minutes
Cooking Time: 35 minutes
Servings: 36
Ingredients

- 1/4 cup light olive oil
- 3/4 cup white sugar
- 2 teaspoons vanilla extract
- 1/2 teaspoon almond extract
- 2 eggs
- 1 3/4 cup all-purpose flour
- 1/4 teaspoon salt
- 1 teaspoon baking powder
- 1/2 cup dried cranberries
- 1 1/2 cup pistachio nuts

Direction

1. Prep oven to 150 ° C
2. Scourge oil and sugar in a large bowl until a homogeneous mixture is obtained. Stir in the vanilla and almond extract and add the eggs. Mix flour, salt, and baking powder; gradually add to the egg mixture — mix cranberries and nuts by hand.
3. Divide the dough in half — form two 12 x 2-inch logs on a parchment baking sheet. The dough can be sticky, wet hands with cold water to make it easier to handle the dough.
4. Bake in the preheated oven for 35 minutes or until the blocks are golden brown. Pullout from the oven and let cool for 10 minutes. Lower oven heat to 275 degrees F (135 degrees C).
5. Cut diagonally into 3/4-inch-thick slices. Place on the sides on the baking sheet covered with parchment — Bake for about 8 to 10 minutes

Nutrition: 92 calories 4.3g fat 2.1g protein

98. Cream Puff Dessert

Preparation time: 20 minutes
Cooking Time: 36 minutes
Servings: 12
Ingredients
Puff

- 1 cup water
- 1/2 cup butter
- 1 cup all-purpose flour
- 4 eggs

Filling

- 1 (8-oz) package cream cheese, softened
- 3 1/2 cups cold milk
- 2 (4-oz) packages instant chocolate pudding mix

Topping

- 1 (8-oz) package frozen whipped cream topping, thawed
- 1/4 cup topping with milk chocolate flavor
- 1/4 cup caramel filling
- 1/3 cup almond flakes

Direction:

1. Set oven to 200 degrees C (400 degrees F). Grease a 9 x 13-inch baking dish.
2. Melt the butter in the water in a medium-sized pan over medium heat. Pour the flour in one go and mix vigorously until the mixture forms a ball. Pull away from heat and let stand for 5 minutes. Beat the eggs one by one until they are smooth and shiny. Spread in the prepared pan.
3. Bake in the preheated oven for 30 to 35 minutes, until puffed and browned. Cool completely on a rack.
4. While the puff pastry cools, mix the cream cheese mixture, the

milk, and the pudding. Spread over the cooled puff pastry. Cool for 20 minutes.

5. Spread whipped cream on cooled topping and sprinkle with chocolate and caramel sauce. Sprinkle with almonds. Freeze 1 hour before serving.

Nutrition: 355 calories 22.3g fat 8.7g protein

99. Fresh Peach Dessert

Preparation time: 30 minutes
Cooking Time: 27 minutes
Servings: 15
Ingredients

- 16 whole graham crackers, crushed
- 3/4 cup melted butter
- 1/2 cup white sugar
- 4 1/2 cups of miniature marshmallows
- 1/4 cup of milk
- 1 pint of heavy cream
- 1/3 cup of white sugar
- 6 large fresh peaches - peeled, seeded and sliced

Direction:

1. In a bowl, mix the crumbs from the graham cracker, melted butter, and 1/2 cup of sugar. Mix until a homogeneous mixture is obtained, save 1/4 cup of the mixture for filling. Squeeze the rest of the mixture into the bottom of a 9 x 13-inch baking dish.
2. Heat marshmallows and milk in a large pan over low heat and stir until marshmallows are completely melted. Remove from heat and let cool.
3. Beat the cream in a large bowl until soft peaks occur. Beat 1/3 cup of sugar until the cream forms firm spikes. Add the whipped cream to the cooled marshmallow mixture.
4. Divide half of the cream mixture over the crust, place the peaches over the cream and divide the rest of the cream mixture over the peaches. Sprinkle the crumb mixture on the cream. Cool until ready

to serve.

Nutrition: 366 calories 22.5g fat 1.9g protein

100. Blueberry Dessert

Preparation time: 30 minutes
Cooking Time: 20 minutes
Servings: 28
Ingredients

- 1/2 cup butter
- 2 cups white sugar
- 36 graham crackers, crushed
- 4 eggs
- 2 packets of cream cheese, softened
- 1 teaspoon vanilla extract
- 2 cans of blueberry pie filling
- 1 package (16-oz) frozen whipped cream, thawed

Direction:

1. Cook butter and sprinkle 1 cup of sugar and graham crackers. Squeeze this mixture into a 9x13 dish.
2. Beat the eggs. Gradually beat the cream cheese, sugar, and vanilla in the eggs.
3. Pour the mixture of eggs and cream cheese over the graham cracker crust. Bake for 15 to 20 minutes at 165 ° C (325 ° F). Cool.
4. Pour the blueberry pie filling on top of the baked dessert. Spread non-dairy whipped topping on fruit. Cool until ready to serve.

Nutrition: 354 calories 15.4g fat 3.8g protein

101. Good Sweet

Preparation Time: 10 minutes
Cooking Time: 10 minutes
Servings: 2
Ingredients:

- Tomatoes, ¼ teaspoon, chopped
- Cucumber, ¼ teaspoon, chopped
- Honey, 2 tablespoons
- Other veggies/beans optional

Directions:

1. Whisk the ingredients well.
2. In a bowl, toss to coat with honey as smoothly as possible.

Nutrition: 187 Calories 15.6g Fat 2g Protein

102. A Taste of Dessert

Preparation Time: 15 minutes
Cooking Time: 0 minutes
Servings: 2
Ingredients:

- Cilantro, 1 tablespoon
- Green onion, 1 tablespoon
- Mango, 1 peeled, seeded and chopped
- Bell pepper, ¼ cup, chopped
- Honey, 2 tablespoons

Directions:
1. Incorporate all the ingredients.
2. Serve when combined well.
Nutrition: 21 Calories 0.1g Fat 0.3g Protein

CONCLUSION

he Mediterranean diet is straightforward, simple, and mouth-watering; your transition to the diet will be a lot smoother and easier if you do a

Tlittle bit of preparation ahead of time.

The health benefit of following the Mediterranean Lifestyle is enormous. It offers well-rounded benefits that encourage optimum physical, emotional, social and mental well-being. No one is as positively charged and healthy as this. Hence, take what you have taken in and kick-start your journey to a great beginning.

No matter if you are taking your first walk down the path of the Mediterranean Lifestyle, or if you are starting to work on a new chapter in your journey, it is essential to have some basic knowledge and tools that will guide you through this process. A little preparation will make all of the difference.

The first thing to do is to clear out anything that contains any kind of unhealthy ingredient or ingredient that you know you don't like. It will be hard at first, but you will get used to it, and over time you won't even think about it.

The next thing to do is to start a food journal. You should keep track of the different ingredients that you are about to add into your diet and the way they make you feel. This way, if one of these ingredients is not good for you, you'll know it right away. That is to say, if you find that you don't feel good after eating pasta, then you will know not to eat it anymore. By doing this, you'll realize that the Mediterranean lifestyle is not only about the food, but also about what we put into our bodies.

Another thing that people usually do wrong is they skip breakfast. Breakfast is a very important meal and should start your day right.

The next thing to do is to set a small goal for you. For example, you can start with drinking a glass of extra virgin olive oil in the morning on an empty stomach. This way, you'll get used to the taste. You should keep track of your goal and how you are feeling each time you reach it.

If this is all too much for you right now, then just start with making one small change at a time until you get used to it.

As long as you do this and stick to the simple rules of a Mediterranean diet, you can attain all the benefits it offers. One of the main benefits of this diet is that it is perfectly sustainable in the long run, not to mention, it is mouth-watering and delicious.

Once you start implementing the various protocols of this diet, you will see a positive change in your overall health. Ensure that you are being patient with yourself and stick to your diet without making any excuses.

Shifting to a new diet making a lifestyle change can be tough! This cookbook will allow you gradually manage this journey and help you understand everything you need to know in this culinary tradition and finally benefit from it in the long run.

CPSIA information can be obtained
at www.ICGtesting.com
Printed in the USA
BVHW061037270521
608294BV00012B/2581